KU-255-327

NARRATIVES OF GUILT AND COMPLIANCE IN UNIFIED GERMANY

In 1992 the files of East Germany's infamous Ministry for State Security, the Stasi, were made publicly available and thousands of former East Germans began to confront their contents. Finally it was possible for ordinary citizens to ascertain who had worked for the Stasi, either on a full-time basis or as an 'unofficial employee', the Stasi's term for an informer. The revelations from these 178 km of documents sparked feuds old and new among a population already struggling through massive social and political upheaval. Drawing upon the Stasi files and upon interviews with one-time informers, this book examines the impact of the Stasi legacy in united Germany.

Barbara Miller examines such aspects of the informer's experience as:

- the recruitment procedure
- daily life and work
- motivation and justification.

She goes on to consider the dealings of politicians and the courts with the Stasi and its employees. Her analysis then turns to the way in which this aspect of recent German history has been remembered, and the phenomenal impact of the opening of the files on such perceptions of the past.

Narratives of Guilt and Compliance in Unified Germany offers important new perspectives on the nature of individual and collective memory and a fascinating investigation of modern German society.

Barbara Miller graduated from the University of Glasgow in 1991 with a degree in German and Psychology. She taught and researched in Germany and Austria before completing her doctoral thesis in Glasgow in 1997. She is now based in Sydney, Australia.

ROUTLEDGE STUDIES IN MEMORY AND NARRATIVE

Series editors: Mary Chamberlain, Paul Thompson, Timothy Ashplant, Richard Candida-Smith and Selma Leydesdorff

1 NARRATIVE AND GENRE
Edited by Mary Chamberlain and Paul Thompson

2 TRAUMA AND LIFE STORIES
International perspectives
Edited by Kim Lacy Rogers and Selma Leydesdorff with Graham Dawson

3 NARRATIVES OF GUILT AND COMPLIANCE IN UNIFIED GERMANY
Stasi informers and their impact on society
Barbara Miller

4 JAPANESE BANKERS IN THE CITY OF LONDON
Junko Sakai

NARRATIVES OF GUILT AND COMPLIANCE IN UNIFIED GERMANY

Stasi informers and their impact on society

Barbara Miller

London and New York

First published 1999
by Routledge
11 New Fetter Lane, London EC4P 4EE

Simultaneously published in the USA and Canada
by Routledge
29 West 35th Street, New York, NY 10001

Typeset in Sabon by Wearset, Boldon, Tyne and Wear
Printed and bound in Great Britain by
MPG Books Ltd, Bodmin

British Library Cataloguing in Publication Data
A catalogue record for this book is available from the British Library

Library of Congress Cataloging in Publication Data

Miller, Barbara, 1969–
Narratives of guilt and compliance in unified Germany : Stasi informers and their impact on society / Barbara Miller.
p. cm.
Includes bibliographical references and index.
ISBN 0–415–20261–2
1. Informers—Germany (East) Biography. 2. Internal security—Germany (East)—History. 3. Germany (East). Ministerium für Staatssicherheit. 4. Germany—Politics and government—1990– I. Title.
HV8210.5.A45M5665 1999
943′.1086′0922—dc21 99–22402
CIP

ISBN 0–415–20261–2

The Germans have a tendency to believe that their ideals are reality.

Helmut Schmidt, former German Chancellor

NOTES ON THE BIBLIOGRAPHY

The references in this book have been compiled from a variety of different sources. To aid the reader, these sources have been divided into categories A–J.

In the text, a reference will first cite this category letter, and then the source number within that category. For instance, (J-63) refers to the reference numbered 63 in the category 'J'. A full list of the Bibliographical Categories is set out below.

A. INTERVIEWS WITH FORMER STASI INFORMERS
B. CORRESPONDENCE
C. STASI FILES
D. STASI DOCUMENTATION
E. SED ARCHIVES
F. ADDITIONAL PRIMARY DOCUMENTATION
G. LAWS
H. PUBLIC DISCOURSE
I. PRESS ARTICLES
J. SECONDARY LITERATURE

CONTENTS

ACKNOWLEDGEMENTS

Two particular incidents come to mind when I look back on teaching work I did on job-training schemes for unemployed East Berliners in the early 1990s. The first was when a man in one group admitted openly to having worked for the Stasi on a full-time basis. An embarrassed silence followed, until someone started to nervously giggle. I stopped asking people what they used to do after that, but on one occasion I brought a newspaper article with me concerning a trial underway against former GDR border-guards. I naïvely imagined that the class would simply be interested in seeing how events in Germany were discussed in the British press. A violent row ensued concerning the relative guilt of the border-guards in question. Many of those in this particular group argued that Chris Gueffroy, the young man who had been fatally wounded in February 1989, had known the danger he faced by attempting to flee the GDR. Occurrences such as these were fascinating, but the issues involved overwhelmed me at the time, and I did not know where to begin and what right I, in an already somewhat controversial role as a 're-trainer', really had to question people about their past lives and about the way in which these lives were being re-shaped and re-defined in their new Germany.

Several years later some of the questions which sparked this initial interest are discussed here, and for this I owe considerable thanks to many people. First and foremost Roddy Watt, for his limitless time and patience, his enthusiastic support and dedication, and for his commas. The continued reassurance of friends and family has also been invaluable in carrying me through the many moments of doubt involved in such an undertaking. I would also like to mention Thomas Rogalla and Helmut Müller-Enbergs of the BStU, whose help ensured that my research took the path it did. Regardless of any moral judgements which the reader might make, this would not have been possible if the ten Stasi informers whose stories are woven throughout this book had not, for whatever reason, been prepared to contribute to this one small part of the confrontation with the Stasi legacy. To them I would also like to extend my sincere thanks.

INTRODUCTION

Beginnings of a societal debate

The collapse of the Berlin Wall on 9 November 1989 signified the end of forty years of inner-German division and indicated that the East/West frontier of Cold War politics, which had been gradually eroded throughout the 1980s, would finally be washed completely from the landscape. The next years were to be witness to massive social and political upheaval in the lands of the former Eastern Bloc, marked by the fragmentation of nation states as a consequence of regional and ethnic conflicts. Events in East Germany did not, however, follow this pattern of segmentation and, on 3 October 1990, less than one year after the jubilant scenes of 9 November, the German Democratic Republic (GDR) and the Federal Republic of Germany (FRG) were politically united. The voices of those who had hoped not for unification, but for a reformed GDR, were drowned by the wave of enthusiasm with which ordinary citizens of the five new federal states initially embraced amalgamation with their more affluent sister state. The GDR had ceased to be, and in the following years the question of how to confront its legacy would become the subject of bitter controversy between and within the two former Germanys.

Assessing forty years of post-war history was never going to be an easy undertaking, and attempts by the legal system to bring the crimes of the former regime to light were criticised for their laxness and ineffectiveness by some, at the same time as they were scorned as exemplifying a form of victor's justice by others. Some prominent West German intellectuals such as Günter Grass argued that the FRG did not have the right to stand in judgement over the GDR (J-31). Frank Schirrmacher of the conservative *Frankfurter Allgemeine* newspaper found fault in this stance, pointing out the irony, as he saw it, that it was precisely those who had been highly critical of the lenient manner in which the crimes of the National Socialist regime had been confronted in the FRG who were suddenly protesting that those who had not been forced to live under the dictatorship did not have the right to judge the actions of those who had (I-13).

Since only one of the two Germanys had ceased to exist, it was ultimately the bulky legacy only of the GDR which would pose so many problems after the initial euphoria of unification had subsided. A substantial proportion of this subsequent reckoning with the GDR past centred around the debate concerning the former Ministry of State Security (the MfS, or, popularly, the Stasi). The decision to make the files of this once so feared organisation publicly available meant that the inhabitants of the former GDR were confronted with harsh realities concerning the extent of their own compliance and conformity. Only a very small minority of East Germans had ever voiced the criticisms of state policies which an increasing number had harboured, at least during the latter years of the GDR's existence. Most had reconciled themselves to the fact, as they saw it, that they would never leave East Germany and had thus suppressed their disapproval of state practices in the desire for a life as free of conflict as possible. By doing so they had helped to ensure the continued existence of the GDR. Once it had ceased to be and its many flaws had been brought to light, this was a stance of which few were particularly proud. It was with a considerable degree of reluctance that many began to face the bitter reality that they had never acted in a manner sufficiently non-conformist to arouse the Stasi's suspicions, particularly since they had perhaps lived their lives believing that the wilful suppression of their true opinion was justified by the fact that they were under Stasi observation.

In the turbulent period immediately following the fall of the Berlin Wall a wave of verbal aggression was directed towards those who had served the MfS, fuelled by the stream of sensational revelations of partly factual, partly fictional Stasi crimes which hit the headlines in the tabloid press. This anger gradually subsided when the considerable material and social concerns resulting from unification began to take precedence in most former East Germans' lives, and after it had been established that the majority of them had not, in fact, ever been under direct surveillance. Yet the issue of how to deal with those whose existence, it was argued, had significantly contributed to an all-prevailing atmosphere of distrust, the Stasi's secret informers, remained very much on the agenda. Defining the relative guilt of these 'unofficial employees', as informers were classified by the Stasi, in a legal context was often extremely difficult and the moral issues involved were equally complex. The injustices which, to varying degrees, had been inflicted upon the population of the GDR had been decreed at higher levels, but those who had been active as Stasi informers had more directly exploited trust by reporting on the activities of friends, neighbours, and even close relatives. Theirs was also a crime which had remained undisclosed until the files were made available, and the banal fascination of the phenomenon of observation and control, combined with the compelling discussion of intricate issues of guilt and compliance within a German context, meant that much debate concerning this unique legacy would focus on these informers.

* * *

On 8 February 1950, legislation was passed in the newly-founded GDR decreeing the creation of an independent Ministry for State Security. Several years later in the aftermath of the events surrounding the workers' revolt of 17 June 1953, Wilhelm Zaisser, the man who had been appointed the first Minister for State Security, was dismissed and the Ministry was temporarily stripped, until 24 November 1955, of its independence and re-integrated into the Interior Ministry. Ernst Wollweber succeeded Zaisser and remained in power until, on 1 November 1957, Erich Mielke took control. Mielke was to occupy the post of Minister for State Security for the next thirty-two years.

The MfS was governed from a central complex in Berlin and served by fifteen district divisions. There is some dispute as to whether the once unquestionably mighty Stasi is best described as having been a state within a state or as 'an instrument used by the SED bureaucracy to retain power' (F-13, p. 5). The more convincing arguments support the latter hypothesis, with more recent work suggesting that, although even the MfS labelled itself the 'Sword and Shield' of the Party, this characterisation alone is too superficial, since it ignores the constantly developing dynamics of the relationship between the Party and the Stasi (J-93).

There is little dispute that over the years the Stasi's foreign espionage department (the HVA) enjoyed considerable success in the FRG. Perhaps most notable was the successful positioning of top spy, Günter Guillaume, in the office of the reigning Chancellor Willy Brandt, whose unmasking was a significant factor in Brandt's decision to relinquish power. What distinguished the Stasi, however, from other Secret Services was the quite substantial amount of resources dedicated to internal affairs (J-22, p. 24). The post-1989 analysis of the documents relating to the Stasi's activities within the GDR has brought the recognition that much of the organisation's attention was focused on specific groups of the population, primarily on individuals associated with the church, with cultural, or with opposition activities. Yet, in the minds of the East German population, the Stasi functioned as though it were physically omnipresent, and many a conversation was subjected to a form of self-imposed censorship in the belief that it was being furtively recorded and analysed.

The numbers of those employed by the Stasi increased steadily throughout the life span of the organisation. In 1974, 55,718 people were employed on a full-time basis, in 1980 there were 75,106 such employees, and by 1989 this figure had risen to 91,000 (J-29, p. 34; J-64, p. 56). Full-time employees were often known among friends and family to be working for the Stasi. For the 174,000 informers estimated to have been active in 1989 this was not the case (J-64, p. 56). The Stasi divided its unofficial employees into several categories, who were each to have varying tasks and areas of responsibility (J-62, pp. 62–90). By far the most common category was the IMS, defined in the 1979 guidelines for the work with informers as follows:

> These are unofficial employees who play a key role in ensuring overall internal security in the area of operation. Their work is generally preventative in nature and they assist in the early detection and implementation of new security requirements. Their work must contribute to the comprehensive and secure evaluation and control of the politically operative situation and help clarify the question of 'Who is who?' (J-62, p. 314).

IME (unofficial employees for a specific purpose) and IMB (unofficial employees who were directly assigned to observe individuals suspected of enemy activities) were, as these definitions indicate, to be given more direct and specific tasks in comparison to the IMS. During the course of contact with the Stasi, the status of unofficial employees could be changed according to their potential to obtain specific information and according to the needs of the Stasi officer concerned. 'Fuchs', for example, was originally recruited as an IMS but was later promoted to an FIM, an unofficial employee who was in charge of other unofficial employees (C-5b, pp. 87–90). When he changed jobs in 1985, 'Fuchs' was once again given the status IMS (ibid. pp. 133–6).

In contrast to the full-time Stasi employees, the majority of unofficial employees did not receive a regular wage for their services, unless they were designated as full-time unofficial employees (J-62, pp. 89–90). By the creation of a cover occupation, care was taken to ensure that the fact that these informers actually worked for the Stasi on a full-time basis remain secret (F-3, pp. 195–6).

Stasi informers were primarily engaged in the amassing of vast amounts of often seemingly trivial pieces of information which could potentially be used to demobilise the enemy (F-3, p. 464). To this aim strategies were devised to destroy or neutralise those whose political stance was perceived as a threat to the smooth running of the state. Much of the vast amount of information collected by the Stasi from its informers was reproduced, often by hand, several times within any given file. When, in 1989, the organisation realised that its days were numbered, measures were put into action to begin the immense task of trying to destroy these screeds of written material. Amidst growing political unrest, the MfS was also renamed the AfNS (Office for National Security) on 17 November 1989 by Hans Modrow, the new leader of the rapidly disappearing GDR, and Wolfgang Schwanitz was appointed head of the reformed organisation (see J-29, 177–292). Less than one month later and under pressure from the Round Table, Modrow's government announced measures to restructure the AfNS into two separate organisations, one responsible for domestic and one for foreign affairs. Finally, the decision was taken to completely disband the MfS/AfNS, leaving a legacy of 178 kilometres of filed material, now in the care of the Federal Commissioner for the Files of the State Security Service of the Former German Democratic Republic (the BStU).

* * *

In the run-up to the events of 1989, the political climate throughout Eastern Europe had been undergoing dramatic change. Once the mood of upheaval had finally reached the GDR, events took on surprising momentum. A significant turning point in this process came in January 1988, when the traditional Rosa–Luxemburg Demonstration ended with the arrest and subsequent forced temporary exile of several leading citizens' rights campaigners. The authorities were enraged when protesters attempted to participate in the march carrying a banner which criticised the State but which displayed a quotation from Luxemburg herself on the nature of freedom (see J-59, pp. 483–553; see also, J-38). Vigils were held for those arrested, and this rally is generally regarded as the first time that previously isolated opposition groups joined together in protest. The mood of dissatisfaction continued to grow, and the obvious rigging of the municipal election results of May 1989 led to a further surge of anti-government sentiment. The situation was now acute, but still few could really have believed that the GDR was heading towards its fortieth and final anniversary, a process which was speeded along by Hungary's decision in late summer 1989 to allow the GDR citizens who had been flocking there the chance to escape into Austria. This decision marked the beginning of a mass exodus from the GDR, and when the Hungarian/Austrian border was finally officially opened on 10 September 1989, 20,000 GDR citizens crossed over into the West in the first few hours alone (J-38, p. 28). In these late summer days, thousands of East Germans had been gathering in foreign embassies in what was then Czechoslovakia and in Poland, and on 30 September the East German authorities allowed the first wave of what amounted to 5,500 refugees in Prague and 800 in Warsaw safe passage to the FRG via specially commissioned trains (ibid. p. 29). International media attention was focused on East Germany, and the emotional images of those who took this opportunity to flee, sometimes even leaving their children behind to do so, were relayed around the world. The stream of those leaving the GDR seemed endless, and celebrations on 7 October 1989 to mark the fortieth anniversary of the Republic were marred when spectators of the parade appealed for help to the visiting Mikhail Gorbachev. The so-called political *Wende* (literally, the turning) was completed when, on 9 November 1989, and after a somewhat confused announcement by leading Party functionary Günter Schabowski, the inner-German border was declared open. The first GDR citizens were allowed by overwhelmed border-guards to cross over to the other side of the Berlin Wall, the barrier which, since its erection in 1961, had symbolised the East/West division.

It was almost a month after the events of the historic night of 9 November 1989 when Stasi offices throughout East Germany were first occupied by members of the public. Activities reached a climax on 15 January 1990 when the headquarters in Berlin were stormed by thousands who had been protesting outside with chants of 'Stasi out' and 'Stasi to work'. Although subsequent reports suggest that the Stasi employees inside were fully prepared for this attack, even to the point of actually opening the doors to the protesting mass outside, the event was immensely symbolic and seemed at the time to signify the final liberation of the *Volk* from its oppressor (see J-109, pp. 33–40). It would later be established that most of the files which literally fell into the hands of the protesters as they ran blindly through the complex were fairly harmless and had been carefully and cunningly placed in their path with the intention of distracting them from going in search of other potentially more explosive material. Agents of the Stasi and possibly even of other Secret Services were very probably taking advantage of the chaotic atmosphere to smuggle more delicate material out of the building.

In the period immediately following this occupation, Stasi officers worked closely with the Citizens' Committee established to oversee the safekeeping of the files. Naturally enough, many of these officers had their own interests at heart in this process and, as a result of their inside knowledge, held a distinct advantage over the members of the committee. Stefan

Wolle later said that he and other members had allowed themselves 'to be led through the labyrinth as though through a museum, without taking command' (J-105, p. 352). The unique nature of the situation meant that many of those who were involved in the ensuing process of disbanding the MfS/AfNS were bound to make what are now seen to be erroneous judgements when carrying out this immense task. Hans Schwenke, who himself was involved in the dissolution process, would later write of this time: 'The Stasi people had their own ideas about how to disband their Secret Service and for a long time played cat and mouse with those engaged in this process' (J-109, p. 218).

Perhaps the most seriously misguided decision made in the period immediately following the storming of Stasi headquarters was the one taken in February 1990 to destroy the electronic data bank which catalogued the material contained in the files. The proposal to take such action was agreed upon by the Round Table, with the justification that the information stored in this bank had been illegally obtained and was potentially exploitable by members of the Stasi or of other Secret Services. With hindsight, this action is recognised by many to have ultimately served only to complicate the ensuing attempt to administer the screeds of documents now in possession of the Gauck Office (the BStU). Soon it was evident that the destruction of material best served the interests of those who had compiled it. The Round Table found itself, however, in an unfortunate position, suffering as it did from a lack of both past experience and of legitimacy (see J-24, p. 77). As a body of representatives from the various political parties and organisations active at the time, many of those who sat at the Round Table wanted to ensure that the principles of democracy were adhered to in this turbulent period. Yet the Round Table was itself a self-appointed and thus undemocratic body, some of whose members, it was later to be revealed, had worked for the Stasi themselves:

> It's like an old joke of history that the first free elections for the East German parliament were organised with the purpose of forming a legislative body whose sole task was to dissolve itself. There's never been anything like it in the history of parliamentary democracies, of all the states to have gone under none of them has done so in such an orderly fashion as the GDR. Just as extraordinary is the fact that at the forefront of the revolution employees of the State Security apparatus were active, whose aim it was to prevent revolutionary changes: de Maizière of the CDU, Ibrahim Böhme of the SPD, Wolfgang Schnur of Demokratischer Aufbruch, to name only the most prominent (J-16, pp. 22–3).

Within, as Wolle described it, the 'bizarre coalition of extreme opposites' which made up the Round Table there were then those who were not so much interested in seeing that justice be done, but rather that their own dealings with the Stasi remained undisclosed. This led Jens Reich to remark that he felt that he and other representatives of the citizens' groups had had the wool pulled over their eyes (J-106, p. 140; I-90).

In spite of the immense difficulties and resistance they faced, the dedication of members of the various citizens' committees resulted in the passing of a law on 24 August 1990 in the East German parliament concerning the protection and use of the data collected by the MfS (G-2). This law ensured that a ruling was included in the Unification Treaty which guaranteed temporary conditions of use until the Stasi Document Law (StUG) was finally passed more than one year later (G-3). This was indeed a significant victory, as many on both sides of the rapidly disappearing German-German border would rather have seen the lid kept firmly shut on this quite extraordinary Pandora's box.

At that time, Germany's StUG was unique in the former Eastern Bloc. In Hungary, for example, legislation was implemented to allow the screening of individuals in specific public positions, but was eventually abandoned in recognition of the fact that there were so few judges available to implement the law who were not themselves liable for screening and possible dismissal (I-93). In Romania the files came under the standard thirty-year closure rule (I-94). The Czech Republic has in the intervening years adopted legislation comparable to the StUG, although this ruling is somewhat less differentiated and intricate than its German counterpart (see J-73, pp. 319–26).

The passing of the Stasi Document Law meant that theoretically an end was in sight to the mass speculation about who had or had not worked for the Stasi. Since its subject matter was so delicate and its implications so potentially grave, the law's specifications were the cause of much heated dispute. According to the StUG (§ 16), for example, former unofficial employees are not granted access to the reports which they wrote or helped compile, with the justification that if they were to be allowed to view this material, 'this reawakened knowledge could be used to the disadvantage of those whom it concerns' (Angelika Barbe, F-16, p. 116). Former Stasi employees may, however, apply to see these sections of the file if they can make the case that the information is required in legal proceedings (StUG, § 16/4).

There was a huge public response to the StUG. In the first three years of the BStU's existence, over 2.7 million applications to view files were lodged (F-17, p. 4). The majority of these requests had come from employers in the public and private sector, but close to one million were private applications from ordinary citizens who wished to know if they had been under Stasi observation. There can be no doubt that in this initial period there was marked public interest in the Stasi legacy. Indeed by mid-1998 the BStU had received no less than 3.87 million applications to see files. Joachim Gauck, the head of the BStU, argues, therefore, that a decision not to confront the harsh truths in the files would have lead to 'an enormous amount of frustration and dissatisfaction' in the East (J-17, p. 91). It is likely that very little of this frustration would have been detectable on the part of those who were active as Stasi informers since they face possible social stigmatisation as well as dismissal from employment if this secret is revealed. Many of these individuals feel that they have been unfairly singled out as scapegoats in the reckoning with the GDR past. Establishing the identities behind the cover names of informers has, however, arguably been a vital part of the confrontation with the Stasi legacy. The task of studying the mechanisms of control would be much impeded if it were not possible to identify those were responsible for devising, implementing and supporting them.

Wolfgang Thierse argued that the emphasis on the informers in the debate over the Stasi legacy was undesirable, that the phenomenon was quite simply 'banal' and should not be sensationalised (J-95, p. 30). He appealed to the general public to stop thinking of former Stasi informers as 'some kind of strange demonic baddies, criminals, swines' but to realise that they were friends, neighbours, and even relatives (ibid.). It is, however, precisely this aspect of the informer network, its banality and the fact that, whether imagined or real, it was a feature of the day-to-day reality of many GDR citizens, which ensures the public's fascination with it.

AIMS AND METHODS

> The unofficial employees are the most important factor in the fight against the secret activities of the class enemy (MfS guidelines/1958, J-62, p. 198).

> The unofficial employees are at the very core of all the Ministry for State Security's politically operative work (MfS guidelines/1968, ibid. p. 247).

> The desired political and social impact of our politically operative

> work is to be achieved by a higher quality and effectiveness of the work with the unofficial employees – the main weapon in the fight against the enemy (MfS guidelines/1979, ibid. p. 305).

After the events of 1989, and particularly after the introduction of the StUG in December 1991, the identities of onetime informers began to be gradually revealed, often in a most spectacular manner. Since very few were prepared on their own initiative to admit to having worked for the Stasi, informers were generally outed after relevant information became available from the Stasi files. As if caught up in some kind of murder mystery game, citizens of the former GDR pondered over the questions of who had done it? by what means? where? and to whom? Two possible explanations of the motivation behind the willingness to work as an unofficial employee were popularly developed and expounded: were the informers evil and sinister individuals who had ruthlessly betrayed their friends and family for their own gain? Or, as many of the unofficial employees themselves began to vehemently claim, were they themselves victims of a brutal system of control whose political *naïveté* had been cunningly abused?

The following chapters will focus predominately on informers who were citizens of the GDR and who were active within its boundaries. Separate guidelines and conditions were in force for those who worked outside the GDR (J-62, pp. 351–61). The opening chapters discuss the personality and social profile of informers, examine why they were selected for this apparently so vital task, what their motivation for agreeing to comply and continuing to work for the Stasi was and what exactly their duties entailed on a day-to-day basis. These first chapters are as much a retrospective analysis as the later ones, since they are concerned not only with the knowledge of the internal workings of the Stasi which the opening of the files has brought, but also with the effect which the post-1989 Stasi debate in the new Germany has had on the way in which a Stasi past is perceived and characterised by both the informers and the society in which they live.

Chapters Five to Ten examine the public and private confrontation with this aspect of GDR history, with respect to the legal and political decision-making concerning dealings with Stasi employees and to the personal and interpersonal reckoning with this issue. How does a society and how does the individual within that society cope with the phenomenon of wide-scale observation and control once the political and legal structures on which the system rested no longer exist? Who decides where guilt lies? In what manner and by whom should it be atoned?

The complex interaction of legal and political issues with social and moral ones is studied throughout by reference in particular to ten life story interviews carried out with Stasi informers, and by an analysis of primary Stasi documentation, including the MfS files of eight of these interviewees.

* * *

In his analysis of the motivation behind the ordinary men of Reserve Police Battalion 101 committing the atrocities they did in World War Two Poland, Christopher Browning concluded that for the men, 'normality itself had become exceedingly abnormal' (J-18, Preface xix). By interviewing the ordinary citizens who had worked as Stasi informers, I hoped to examine whether the above statement could also be applied to this group and to discover how they themselves viewed their actions, both at the time when they were active for the Stasi and retrospectively from within the context of unified Germany.

Interviews were carried out with seven men and three women, whose ages ranged from 34 to 66. Two of these interviewees had answered a small classified advertisement which appeared in the *Junge Welt*, formerly the newspaper of the GDR's youth organisation, the FDJ. The advertisement appeared on 1 October 1994 and read as follows: 'British researcher seeks former unofficial employees to discuss the confrontation with the Stasi past. Discretion assured.' A further six interviewees were selected from the responses to an article which appeared in the *Märkische Allgemeine Zeitung*, published in Potsdam (I-30). This article had generated a total of twenty-three responses, thirteen from former informers, and a further ten from full-time MfS employees and from individuals who had themselves been informed upon. I approached the ninth interviewee, Kerstin Kaiser-Nicht ('Katrin'), directly. Kaiser had gained a seat in the German parliament representing the PDS (the follow-on party to the SED) after the 1994 elections and was the only one of the interviewees who was a publically-known figure. Although she had made the fact of her previous Stasi connections known before the elections, Kaiser was accused of not having been entirely honest about the details and extent of these contacts and was eventually pressurised by her own party, as well as by opposing political factions, into resigning her mandate. The tenth interview took place with Berthe Zulind (a pseudonym), alias 'Sonnenblume', whom I contacted after reading the account of her Stasi past in her autobiography (J-110). By examining predominantly cases of those who were not public figures, and who could be assured that what they said would be treated in confidence, I hoped that a more open dialogue would be facilitated. I suspected that those informers whose cases had been prominent in the media would be so practised at answering certain typical questions regarding their Stasi past that they would have built up a repertoire of set answers. This was confirmed when, at times during my conversation with 'Katrin', I could not shake the feeling that I might as well be listening to a tape recorded account of her past life. A certain lack of restraint on the part of those to whom I spoke may also have resulted from the fact that I was a foreigner, a complete outsider, to whom my interviewees seemed to attribute political neutrality.

I went to the homes of nine of the interviewees and to the office of one of them, 'Thaer'. Although I explained to my interview partners that they should feel free to ask me to stop recording at any time if they felt uncomfortable, only one man did in the end ask me not to record a few select details of his story. I did not listen to any of the tape recordings until I had spoken to all ten people. After I had begun to work with the taped material I contacted most of the informers again and asked them to clarify and expand on certain details. Only after this point had been reached did I view the Stasi files. These files were available for eight of the ten former unofficial employees. I was not granted access to the file of 'Thaer', the one West German with whom I spoke. In 1993 'Thaer' had been charged with spying for a foreign power and had received a fine and probationary sentence. Unfortunately the files relating to this case, I was informed, were subject to the Secrecy Act (B-5). It is likely that the work of the other person for whom no material was available, 'Wolfgang', had come under the auspices of the Stasi's foreign espionage department, the HVA. The HVA was granted permission in the immediate post-Wall period to disband itself. Much of the material relating to foreign espionage has consequently disappeared, been destroyed or put under lock and key in Washington and Moscow.

The Stasi divided files relating to unofficial employees into two main sections. In the *Personalakte*, Personal File, biographical details of the unofficial employees were recorded, along with those of their immediate family. Documentation regarding the selection and recruitment of the informers was also stored here, as well as other general information, such as details of any reward received for services rendered. The second part of the file was termed the *Arbeitsakte*, Work File, and it was here that the reports of the meetings were filed. The Personal File and the Work File could have various volumes, depending on the length and intensity of the work carried out.

In addition to the files relating to specific individuals, general Stasi documentation, such as the guidelines for the work with unofficial employees, drawn up in 1958, 1968 and 1979, are often cited here (J-62). Although the formal procedure laid down in the guidelines was not always adhered to, the guidelines are fundamental to an understanding of the theoretical structure of the informer network.

Material stemming from the MfS's *Juristische Hochschule* (JHS), School of Law, the euphemism under which the Stasi's own college operated, is also cited. The material originating from the JHS falls into two categories – pedagogic material used in the training of Stasi officers, and the results of research undertaken at the JHS. The pedagogic material may be regarded as being comparable in content to the informer guidelines, that is as theoretical statements of the desired procedure. These works will of course have been shaped by Stasi ideology. Nevertheless, they are still valuable, since they allow insight into the issues of the informer system which were addressed by the Stasi in its own research. They are particularly interesting when they demonstrate that certain aspects of the daily work with informers often did not follow the strict format laid down in the guidelines.

THE STASI FILES: FACT OR FICTION?

> The files are a dangerous mixture of fact and fiction.
>
> (Vera Wollenberger, J-107, p. 162)

After the turbulent events of 1989/90 and the subsequent dissolution of the Stasi, there were many appeals for the destruction of the organisation's files. Although he later claimed not to have meant it literally, prominent clergyman Friedrich Schorlemmer was quoted as suggesting that a huge bonfire be made with the documents (I-23). Even the then reigning Chancellor Helmut Kohl seemed to advocate that the files be disposed of, stating that they were an annoyance and a source of evil rumours (I-63). Such arguments were often heard from those who themselves had worked for the Stasi and who now claimed that the documents were inaccurate and misleading. At one of a series of public discussions in the museum at Checkpoint Charlie, one former Stasi officer claimed: 'Even if it says there that the informer "Dirk" or whoever said this and that, that doesn't necessarily mean that he did' (H-1). Manfred Stolpe, Brandenburg's Premier, was of a similar opinion, arguing that the files did not correspond to the whole truth, 'and a half truth can have the same effect as a complete lie' (I-42, p. 32). Stolpe suggested that it was possible to analyse the information contained in the files only in conjunction with the statements of those who had been present (ibid.). It was indeed no surprise that Stolpe held this view since in the debate surrounding his extensive Stasi contacts the overwhelmingly pro-Stolpe testimonies of numerous politicians and theologians from both East and West were undoubtedly a key factor in ensuring that his name was cleared.

Arguing against the destruction of the Stasi files, the historian Armin Mitter pointed out that no one would ever conceive of burning chronicles from the Middle Ages simply because there was mention of divine miracles in them (I-11). Mitter argued that the files should be treated with the same distanced objectivity applied to any historical source. Yet, one crucial difference between the Stasi files and other comparable historical legacies is that the fates of those who compiled the documents which spoke of heavenly intervention have, in contrast to those of the authors of the Stasi files, long since been decided. The extraordinary decision to make these documents immediately accessible necessarily resulted in dealings with their contents being very much more sensitised than might have been the case if a customary period of closure had been imposed.

In the hysteria which, at least initially, surrounded the confrontation with the Stasi legacy, a critical analysis of the information released by the BStU often did not take place, leading the writer turned PDS politician Stephan Heym to observe that the information found there was being treated 'as if it had come straight from the Bible' (J-36, p. 74). Heym was personally doubtful of the validity of texts which had been compiled by informers who, he argued, were rewarded by the number and length of reports given, and by Stasi officers, whose welfare was dependent on the number of informers in their charge (ibid.). It is certainly the case, as Heym suggests, that throughout the Stasi's lifespan unofficial employees were all too often recruited on the basis of quantity rather than quality, a fact of which Stasi boss Mielke was critically aware (J-62, pp. 93–6). A few cases are also documented where Stasi officers literally invented so-called 'fictitious unofficial employees'. Evidence suggests, however, that these incidents were few and far between and when discovered had serious repercussions for the officer concerned (J-62, pp. 140–1; F-4, p. 66). That it is simply not the case that a mass of unwitting individuals was registered as informers is confirmed by the fact that in almost every single case of someone having been identified through the files as having worked for the Stasi, this person has sooner or later admitted that this was the case.

The Stasi could never have functioned as it did if it had been constantly fed erroneous and fabricated information. In order to ensure that the information received was 'true, complete, current, original and testable' it was to be checked and double-checked (F-3, p. 171). Such extensive verification was possible since informers were not evenly distributed among the population but rather, according to the Focusing Principle, concentrated in areas of suspected subversive activity. This working principle meant that reports from any one informer could be compared with those of others active in the same circles. In this sense the Stasi increasingly tested and re-tested the reliability of its sources, rather as a historical researcher might do (J-22, p. 33). It was thus difficult for any one informer to be consistently untruthful. 'Fuchs', for example, tried to disguise the fact that he was still in contact with an old friend who lived in the FRG. Unbeknown to 'Fuchs', a second friend, who actually functioned as the link to the man in the West, was also registered as an informer, and this man informed his Stasi officer whenever there was communication between 'Fuchs' and his friend in the West. This information found its way through the MfS's internal channels to 'Fuchs's' Stasi officer and was noted (C-5a, p. 229). 'Stephana' was equally unsuccessful in her attempt to deceive the Stasi. 'Stephana' told her new boyfriend that she had contacts to a representative from the Stasi and in doing so broke the oath taken to remain silent about her work. She was, at least at this point, unaware that her new boyfriend was also active as an informer and had reported the story to his Stasi officer, who promptly passed this information on (C-6a, pp. 102–12).

Just as it was not easy to keep facets of one's private life hidden from the Stasi, it could prove equally futile to fabricate information concerning others. Information which was judged significant usually required verification by various sources before it was acted upon. This is not to say that every individual piece of information which an informer gave approached some sort of objective reality, rather that the general character of the work carried out may usually be deduced from any one informer's file. Caution must, of course, always be exercised, particularly when the reports of the meetings have been written up well after the fact by the Stasi officer. The Stasi was indeed aware of potential discrepancies between the content of the actual meeting and that of the report, and later guidelines underline the importance of obtaining written reports from informers to try and combat this problem (see J-22, pp. 36–7). The fact that the Stasi knew of and was keen to eradicate such flaws in the system is further underlined by the following complaint made by Mielke in 1971 concerning the work with informers:

> Even indications or signs of dishonesty, unreliability, betrayal of the code of silence, refusal to cooperate, or other suspicious phenomena, which in some units are found in almost 10 per cent of cases, have not led to in-depth investigations (F-5, I, 307).

The Stasi carried out routine spot checks on its informers and full-time employees, and although Mielke seems to have considered the degree of dishonesty high, it was clearly detected in only a minority of all cases.

Even in the incidents mentioned by Mielke it may well have been the case that the informers were guilty not of inventing information about others, but rather, as in the above examples from 'Fuchs' and 'Stephana', that they had been untruthful about details of their personal lives. The argument that the average informer did not simply fabricate the majority of the information given to the MfS is supported by a comment from the writer Reiner Kunze, who, when describing the, by all accounts, extraordinary Ibrahim Böhme, claimed that he was 'different from all the other informers in my file. He created a world of his own with real people. And then he manipulated them.' (J-49, p. 117).

There is undoubtedly a degree of inconsistency and inaccuracy in the files, yet to propose that the documents ought to be destroyed on these grounds ignores the fact that in the debate surrounding former Stasi informers the controversial issue has often been less the relative truth content of the reports which an informer helped compile, but rather more commonly the question of whether this person was or was not aware that they were registered by the Stasi as an unofficial employee.

The balance of fact or fiction in the files is an issue which not only affects dealings with former unofficial employees but is one with which those who were under Stasi observation have also been very much concerned. The inaccuracies or misconstructions of their life histories as they remember them did not weaken the resolve of the citizens' rights groups to keep the files open. Reiner Kunze did, however, advocate that a clause (§ 14) be included in the StUG allowing individuals like himself to have their files destroyed if they so wished: 'I reject the notion that it should once again be up to me to prove that a lie is a lie. That's what I've had to do all my life' (F-16, p. 216).

The question of whether the relative truth content of the information in the files should be a consideration when it is made public received varying responses in German courts of law. Paragraph 34/2 of the StUG specifies that if an individual considers information published from the files to be false then they have the right to make a counter declaration which must be printed alongside any subsequent publications of the material. When Reiner Kunze was taken to court by fellow writer, Hermann Kant, for having published extracts from his file which showed Kant in an unfavourable light and whose validity Kant contested, Kunze won the case. The court ruled that, in keeping with the StUG, it was Kant's right to ensure that in the future his counter declaration was printed with the material, but that ultimately:

> The publication of a Stasi file is an important contribution to the current debate. There is considerable public interest in such

> material (StG, § 193). It cannot therefore be made mandatory that the validity of every statement in a file is checked before it is published. It is thus up to the person who contests its validity to prove their case (J-3, p. 349).

Not all legal decisions concerning the publication of information from the Stasi files were based on the principles applied in the above case. Members of the political party, the Neues Forum in Halle, were dismayed to find themselves losing several court battles after having made allegedly anonymously-donated lists of former Stasi employees available for public viewing. Although, in this case, checks by the BStU indicated that the information was factually accurate, it was ruled that the right of the public to the information did not outweigh the individual rights of those whose names appeared on the lists (I-27). In the Kant/Kunze case it was decided that the material was of public interest almost regardless of its relative truth content. The members of the Neues Forum were in contrast found to have acted unlawfully in making material public even when it could be shown to be factually accurate.

Historian Roger Engelmann argues that the legacy of the Stasi files is of key importance in the confrontation with the GDR past for three principle reasons. First because the Stasi, in comparison to other Secret Services, was a relatively large apparatus whose legacy, at 178 kilometres of filed material, was not depleted to the same extent as the files, for example, of the National Socialist regime. Second, the area in which the Stasi was active, as was the case for the other Secret Services in Eastern Europe, was more extensive than that of traditional secret police. Third, the amount of written documentation is unusually high and was, furthermore, often compiled according to precise regulations (J-22, p. 24).

In summary, the Stasi acquired and documented vast amounts of information which its officers relied upon to construct operational plans. Before any action was taken, information deemed significant was generally confirmed from a number of informers whose identities often remained unknown to one another. Reports supplied by informers could not be easily fabricated as this might have been detected, and if such incidents had been all too commonplace, the network of Stasi spies would have been unable to function at all. A certain degree of inaccuracy and ideological influence is undoubtedly to be found in the files, and Karl Wilhelm Fricke emphasised that although it was highly unlikely that information had been simply invented, since it formed the basis of the Stasi's operations, the possibility should not be eliminated that the files were sometimes 'beautified' (F-13, p. 79). On the basis of arguments such as these I will end the consideration of the relative truth content of the MfS files, as is relevant here, with the conclusion and caution contained in the final report of the Enquete Commission, the parliamentary committee set up to examine aspects of the GDR regime and its legacy:

> As far as has so far been established the reports of the MfS stand in contrast to the glorified reports of the SED and the other political parties and organisations. After all the State Security Service had the task of realigning politically dangerous voices in the population and dealing with any security risks. Researchers will always have to differentiate between ideological statements and statements upon which operational decisions were taken, as well as determining the relationship of these two elements to one another (F-1, pp. 227–8).

1

'A COMPLETELY NORMAL BIOGRAPHY'? (A-3)

The extensive surveillance and control measures implemented by the Stasi involved being constantly aware and informed of which individuals posed a threat to internal security at any one time, in other words asking the key question of 'Who is who?' (F-3, p. 286). A so-called OPK surveillance measure was often implemented to this aim. An OPK had three main applications: to confirm or reject suspicions that an individual had acted unlawfully; to identify individuals who were negatively disposed towards the state; or to screen individuals who held positions of power potentially open to misuse (ibid.). An OPK sometimes led to an OV, the next and more intensive stage of surveillance. Informers were to establish or to exploit already existing contacts to individuals who were being observed under an OV, so aiming to obtain information which was of 'operative significance'. An essential part of any OV was the concept of *Zersetzung*, literally the decomposition of perceived enemies, achieved by implementing measures to 'split up, lame and de-stabilise' them (ibid. p. 464).

The work of the Stasi's informers, the unofficial employees, was central to the planning and execution of the measures outlined above. In 1989, 174,000 such employees were registered as active. Overall numbers had decreased slightly during the 1980s after rising steadily throughout the previous two decades (F-10, p. 11). Estimated at approximately 10 per cent per annum, there was a fairly high annual turnover of informers (ibid. p. 8). In some district divisions the figure may have been higher. One division, for example, recorded an annual turnover of 18 per cent (D-4, I, p. 43).

Females were not highly represented in the Stasi's network of unofficial helpers. Eighty to ninety per cent of informers were male, and there were no female Stasi officers in charge of informers at all (I-33). It is not clear why the percentage of women informers should have been so low or why 'particular care' was to be taken in dealings with them (J-62, p. 271). There seems to be no evidence that women made less competent informers than men. The low percentage of female informers may simply reflect patriarchal structures within the SED and Stasi. Perhaps there was also concern that officers might become intimately involved with the females in their charge and so run the risk of betraying confidential information. Mielke, at least, seemed to be in favour of increasing the number of female informers working for him. Women, he felt, had shown themselves to be capable of the task at hand and should be actively recruited, particularly as IMV (F-5, I, p. 288). IMV, who were later referred to as IMB, were unofficial employees directly assigned to observe individuals suspected of enemy activity (J-62, p. 258). It is likely that Mielke considered women to be particularly suited as IMV since they could potentially form intimate relationships with these suspected state enemies. These bonds could be fruitful for extracting information, or their very existence could potentially be used for blackmailing purposes. Indeed, earlier guidelines suggest that 'young, good-looking, female unofficial employees with good manners, the ability to pick things up quickly and who are able on account of their professional position to form connections to specific social groups' should be recruited as informers (ibid. p. 203).

Informers were thus not distributed evenly among the population but were recruited according to the Focusing Principle, defined in the Stasi's dictionary of key terms as follows:

> Focusing Principle – important basic principle of the politically operative work and the management thereof aimed at guaranteeing that actions aimed at clarifying and combatting all subversive enemy attacks are goal-oriented and preventative in nature – and are achieved by concentrating all operative forces and means, including the time, technical and financial resources available, on the most important areas of operation, that is on those objects, areas, territories, groups and individuals where preventative security measures are required (F-3, pp. 374–5).

In accordance with this principle informers were more concentrated in cultural groups, in church-based organisations and in opposition groups. The ratio of informers to non-informers could be fairly high in such groups, but in line with the principle that 'each individual is only given as much information as he requires to fulfil his duties' those working for the Stasi were generally unaware of each other's identity and were perhaps not even aware that other informers were active in their immediate environment (F-3, p. 129). Informers were thus often reporting on one another as much as on those individuals being observed in an OPK or OV. The sheer density of informers occasionally made it difficult for a Stasi officer to ensure that those in his care did not become aware of one another's identity. On one occasion, when the writer Rainer Schedlinski was meeting with his Stasi officer in a car park, he suddenly caught sight of another writer, Sascha Anderson, coming in their direction and quickly took cover. Unbeknown to Schedlinski, Anderson was also active as an informer for the Stasi and was working with the same officer. It later transpired that Anderson had spotted Schedlinski and realised that he must also be working for the Stasi. When Anderson reported this incident to his officer, the latter confirmed that this was the case, but asked Anderson to keep Schedlinski in the dark about the matter (J-2, pp. 248–9).

Since the most successful unofficial employee was clearly going to be someone who had contacts with the enemy, it was more practical for the Stasi to recruit from within opposition circles rather than to try to infiltrate them. This led to the paradoxical situation that many informers were reporting on the activities of opposition groups with which they simultaneously worked. The policy of the Stasi towards these individuals was at times somewhat illogical and ambivalent. 'Stephana', for example, was asked on several occasions to break off the contact she had to a man who had applied to leave the GDR. She was warned that such contacts were undesirable and that if she continued to pay no heed to the cautions she could not expect the Stasi's support if she were to get into difficulties (C-6b, I, pp. 266, 325, 390). Since 'Stephana' was reporting on the activities of a man who was under surveillance, it seems to make no sense to suggest to her that contact with such an individual was to be avoided. Perhaps, in this case, logic decreed that the unofficial employee should have contact with the enemy, but ideology confounded this logic, causing Stasi officers to become uneasy when the bond between the informer and the individual under observation appeared to be one of genuine friendship. This contradiction between the Stasi's policy and practice is evident throughout the life span of the organisation. Guidelines from 1952 concerning recruitment emphasise that in order to most effectively combat enemy groups it is necessary to recruit informers who will win the trust of such groups most easily: 'These are former fascists, officers of the fascist army, relatives of agents in custody, criminal and corrupt individuals, morally depraved youths, so-called political refugees etc.' (J-62, p. 166). This extract is in line with the Focusing Principle. The guidelines from 1958 state, however, that political conviction is to be the most important and frequently employed basis for recruitment (ibid. p. 212). Although apparently contradictory, the co-existence of the Focusing Principle and the stipulation that political conviction should be the principal motive for recruitment can perhaps be explained by the fact that the Stasi, wishing to uphold its own ideology, hoped to be able to convince 'corrupt' and 'depraved' individuals of the political necessity of co-operation (ibid. p. 166). Indeed the 1968 guidelines explicitly stipulate that SED members are only to be recruited as informers in exceptional cases since it was felt that such individuals were already committed to actively supporting the State (ibid. p. 261). Before recruiting such an individual Stasi officers were asked to consider whether it would not suffice to give this person the status of a *GMS*, a person who periodically supplied the MfS with information but to whom contact was less formalised and less secretive (J-62, p. 261). All too often Stasi officers ignored this ruling and swelled the ranks of the informer network with Party members, who tended to be relatively easy to recruit. Such practice led Mielke to complain that in many regional divisions as many as one in three newly recruited informers belonged to the SED (F-5, II, p. 440). A Stasi study by Seidler and Schmidt from 1968 put the figure even higher, at 40.7 per cent (D-6, I, p. 7). Interestingly, five of the ten informers with whom I carried out interviews had been a member of the SED and a higher proportion, seven, reported having voted for the PDS, the follow-on party to the SED.

* * *

Individuals were theoretically only to be selected for recruitment as informers when they could satisfy an already existing need. This need was expressed in a Requirement Profile. A Requirement Profile specified a particular need, and identified, in terms of experience, ability and personality characteristics, the type of person who might be suitable for this task (J-62, p. 341).

In reality, many informers were recruited because it proved relatively easy to do so rather than because there was a specific task at hand for them to carry out. Some Requirement Profiles seem furthermore to have been put together with a particular person in mind. Mielke was critical of such practice, complaining: 'You can't just recruit any old unofficial employee and check later what roll he can fulfil' (F-5, II, p. 581). In the following three cases there does, however, seem to have been an existing need, as defined by a Requirement Profile. 'Sonnenblume' was recruited because of her suspected involvement with a 'Criminal Smuggling Ring', the Stasi's definition for those engaged in activities to try to help people leave the GDR (C-8a, p. 65). In 'Stephana's' case, the Stasi was interested in recruiting someone who had contacts to various religious groups, a Requirement Profile which she fitted perfectly (C-6a, p. 14). The third example concerns 'Fuchs', who was recruited as an FIM in order that he could build up a network of informers among the inmates of the prison where he worked (C-5a, p. 80).

Regardless of the specifics of the Requirement Profile, all unofficial employees were in theory to have considerable interpersonal skills in order to successfully carry out the required duties. One study from the Stasi college names, among others, the following desired qualities for all informers:

> The ability to assess situations
> The ability to fully comprehend the political and ideological content and consequences of events
> The ability to judge human character and behaviour
> The ability to form and preserve relationships based on trust
> The ability to observe and take in information on situations and people in a planned and concentrated manner, over a short or long time, as well as the ability to retain and reproduce this information as quickly as possible
> The ability to cope with high demands and burdens and to deal with individual doubts and scruples (D-4, I, pp. 140–6).

Finding candidates who fulfilled all the above requirements cannot have been easy, and the authors of the study do concede that it is not to be expected that an informer possess all these qualities at the time of recruitment. Some of them were to be developed in the course of the work with the Stasi (ibid. I, 148). In the documentation relating to recruitment Stasi officers tended, however, to emphasise the positive characteristics of the candidates rather than identifying the skills or abilities which needed to be developed. 'Fuchs', for example, was considered a suitable candidate because of his ability to understand people and to make accurate observations (C-5a, p. 76). He was also praised for his dedication at work: 'His efforts to find and apply the best possible didactic methods under prison conditions are worthy of mention' (ibid.). 'Stephana' was thought to be particularly suited for the role of an unofficial employee as a result of the fact that she was 'outgoing', 'ambitious' and 'conscientious' (C-6a, p. 34). It is rather ironic that in order to carry out this most deceitful of tasks, the Stasi sought out individuals who were thought to have such positive qualities, including, ironically, a 'well-developed sense of justice' (J-62, p. 266).

Although there are certain general characteristics which can be applied to the population of informers, it is clear that the Stasi was successful in recruiting a wide range of personalities to work in this role. The use of the oral testimonies of individual informers was particularly illuminating in this context since the unprecedented decision to make the files of the GDR's Secret Service so widely accessible meant that the statements of those interviewed could be directly compared and contrasted with the information contained in the Stasi documents relating to these same individuals. Furthermore, since the files have not been subject to a standard closure rule, the likelihood that witnesses were both alive and traceable was greatly increased. Through examination of convergence and divergence between the two sources, a wider perspective of external events is gained, as well as the chance to analyse the perception and interpretation of these same occurrences on the part of the individual informer. In the following introduction to the ten informers whose stories are referred to throughout this book, some biographical details have, in some cases, been changed.

'ROLF'

'Rolf' was born in 1952 in a small town in Saxony. After leaving school he studied agriculture, returning to his hometown in 1979 to take up a post in the museum there, which he held until 1991. During this time he completed a degree in biology by distance learning.

As a young man, 'Rolf' reports having been somewhat negatively disposed towards the State. He had the impression that all his mail at the boarding school he attended was being checked, and this bothered him intensely. As he grew older, his attitudes began to change. Although he was not a member of the SED, 'Rolf' increasingly felt that he should support the State he lived in. He was a keen supporter of environmental issues and one of the reasons he came to the Stasi's attention was because of the contacts he had with environmentalists in the West.

When I visited him, 'Rolf' was obviously nervous, yet eager to talk. His wife sat in on most of our conversation, and his 18-year-old son, his only child, came and listened quietly for a short time. 'Rolf' seemed a shy man, perhaps a little naïve, and someone who was making an apparently genuine attempt to face up to his past. This was reflected, among other things, in the open family atmosphere regarding his Stasi connections and in the fact that he was the only person with whom I spoke who would have been prepared to have been referred to by his real name here.

In 1993 'Rolf' made his Stasi connections publicly known to the local council of which he was a member. He had hoped that such a revelation would lead to an enlightened debate in this forum and was disappointed when it did not. Yet he felt personally unable to take the initiative and begin such a discussion. The news of his Stasi past appeared in the local press shortly afterwards. He was astounded to discover that the only person to broach the topic with him was an old school friend who was visiting the town at the time. At work, none of his wife's colleagues discussed the matter with her either. Although confused by this public reaction, 'Rolf' feels relieved that he has overcome the hurdle of making his past public and feels that the matter is now largely settled.

Whilst active as an informer 'Rolf' found that he could not overcome his scruples about reporting on an acquaintance of his, Michael Beleites. 'Rolf' approached Beleites and confessed his Stasi connections, whereupon Beleites asked if 'Rolf' would be prepared to try and help him plot against the Stasi. Beleites hoped that if he and 'Rolf' were to jointly compile reports in which Beleites was presented as someone who did not pose a threat to internal security, the Stasi might relax the ban from travelling outside the GDR which had been imposed upon him. In the book Beleites later wrote documenting his observation by the Stasi, a short account appears by 'Rolf' describing his time as an informer (J-6, pp. 196–8). Beleites praises 'Rolf' in the book for his willingness to endanger himself by agreeing with his plan: 'By trying to help me in this way, he showed more courage and character than many of the "innocent" people who had no contact to the Stasi' (ibid. p. 193).

When I last heard from 'Rolf' he was working on a freelance basis at his hometown museum again and considering applying for a new job as the head of a recently-opened nature park. He was aware of the fact that his Stasi past might hinder his chances on the job market, but felt that the Stasi hysteria had subsided enough for his case to be viewed objectively (B-1).

'THEODOR'

On the phone 'Theodor' seemed rather confused and nervous, so it was quite a shock to meet the composed, polite, and articulate man behind the voice. During our conversation he periodically became excited and animated, but remained ultimately in control of the situation, never, it seemed, giving away any more than he intended to.

'Theodor' expanded on his family background in great detail. His father had been an officer in the First and Second World Wars and had worked as a banker in the Weimar Republic. The end of World War Two had thus signalled the second great defeat in the life of 'Theodor's' father. Once again the system he had actively supported had crumbled. Comparing his own situation in united Germany, 'Theodor' felt that he could now empathise with his father.

Born in the 1930s, 'Theodor' says that as a young boy he was deeply shocked by and ashamed of Germany's war crimes, and so embraced life in the GDR as a true alternative to fascism. He describes himself as having 'a more than average respect for authority' and joined the army after leaving school (A-2). He claims to have initially loathed military life, but, since he had committed himself to ten years' service, would have been unable to stand the humiliation of leaving before this time. When he became a communications officer, life improved immensely for 'Theodor'. He was often working with highly motivated trainees, and he found the research projects he was involved in stimulating. It was during this period that he was active as an informer, according to the information in his file from 1975 until 1985. Interestingly, he writes in his first letter to me that his time with the Stasi spanned the period from approximately 1972 until 1986 (B-2). Since there could be no advantage to his claiming that he was active as an informer for longer than was actually the case, it would seem that this miscalculation on his part is evidence that individuals do have trouble remembering the exact details of their contact with the MfS, if not its general nature (see Chapter 9).

'Theodor' retired from his job in the wake of unification out of the fear that if he did not do so his Stasi connections would become public and he would be dismissed. He now lives with his family in Brandenburg.

'FALKE'

'Falke', who was born in the late 1940s, described his biography as having been 'completely normal' (A-3). His mother was a housewife and his father a bricklayer. Since he did well at school, he was able to complete his school leaving certificate and remembers having been the only child from a true working-class background in his class. After three years in the army he joined the police force and, in 1971, began work with the criminal investigation department. During this time he undertook further studies and feels that he had a lot of success in his work.

'Falke' related the details of his biography at the same high speed and with the same apparent brusque detachment with which he carried out the whole interview. In many ways he incorporated all the characteristics of the archetypal remorseless informer, unprepared to admit to any feelings of guilt whatsoever and tending rather to wallow in self-pity about his present situation. Previously a man with an important job, he had been dismissed from his post as a Senior Criminal Investigator in 1993 when screening revealed that he had been active as a Stasi informer from 1977 until 1989. 'Falke' had denied such contacts when asked on the questionnaire concerning previous connections to the Stasi which, as a public service employee from the GDR, he had been required to complete. To me he came across as rather a sad figure, taking his dog for a walk in his track suit, too old to begin again and too young to be content in this unexpected early retirement.

'REINER'

When I asked 'Reiner' at the beginning of our conversation to tell me about his childhood, schooling etc., he took some time before getting around to doing so, first and foremost emphasising his lack of guilt and his belief that 'life' had determined his biography (A-4). 'Reiner' did not seem to want to talk at length about his Stasi past at any point in our meeting, but rather to dwell on almost any other topic. He requested that we take a break from recording on several occasions and evidently found having me in the house quite exciting. He told me about a holiday he had once won, about his weekend cottage and the squirrel he often fed there, but relatively little about the Stasi. Throughout the interview 'Reiner' became, however, increasingly direct and to the point when talking of the public confrontation with the Stasi legacy. He had very firm opinions about the way things should have been in the GDR and was bitter about much of what had happened since unification, feeling that the people from the East were being as badly treated in united Germany as they had been under Honecker.

'Reiner' was born in 1931 in Pomerania. When he was one-year-old he was entrusted to the care of foster parents with whom he spent a happy childhood. At the end of the war his family was forced to flee his hometown. They moved to Magdeburg, where 'Reiner' trained as a mechanic after leaving school. His adoptive parents had been relatively old when they took him in, and both died shortly after the end of the war. Around this time the police force was actively recruiting and 'Reiner' decided to join up since he had no family or other commitments. He worked in Berlin as a motorbike policeman for some years, before returning to Magdeburg when he married a local woman. Back home, he initially worked with the fire brigade and, in 1955, joined the Criminal Police, with whom he remained employed until the early 1970s. By this time 'Reiner' had become disillusioned with the atmosphere at work and had been trying to resign for some time. In a lengthy declaration as to the reasons why he wanted to terminate his employment he wrote:

> There is an impersonal atmosphere in the district headquarters – not the combative atmosphere necessary to fulfil the given tasks. I see the reasons for this situation as resulting from the fact that throughout the 1960s there has been a steady decrease in critical appraisal and self-evaluation (C-4a, I, p. 120).

The advantageous circumstance that 'Reiner' wished to leave his job was exploited to recruit him as a full-time unofficial employee in charge of other unofficial employees, an HFIM. He continued to work in this capacity until a series of health complaints compelled him to retire from this full-time status in the 1980s. 'Reiner' continued contact with the Stasi as a regular unofficial employee until 1989.

'THAER'

'Thaer' was the only person from the FRG to whom I spoke. In 1992 he had been tried for foreign espionage and given a two-year probationary sentence and a fine. As previously mentioned, I was unable to gain access to any Stasi documentation relating to 'Thaer'. I had the feeling that the details of his story were considerably more complex than he was prepared to reveal. Since I had only his word to go on, there was, however, no way of estimating how much he chose to leave out or gloss over in his account.

'Thaer' was born in the late 1940s in a small town near Hamburg. The family later moved to Bavaria and then, in 1963, to Berlin. Here 'Thaer' took up his studies in agriculture. He had originally toyed with the idea of a career in development work in the Third World, but by the time he had graduated the job prospects for such work no longer looked so rosy. He began to work for an organisation called the Farmer's Union. It was during this time that 'Thaer's' contacts with the Stasi began. These contacts were maintained even after he changed jobs, and he was still active as an informer in 1989. When I met him, 'Thaer' was living in Brandenburg and had set up his own business, offering a bulk buying service to small agricultural holdings.

Sadly, in Spring 1998 I was contacted by his sister who informed me that 'Thaer' had passed away suddenly a few months previously.

'FUCHS'

In his original letter 'Fuchs' described his biography as having being 'not spectacular, but certainly typical for a former East German' (B-7). When I met him I told him that if he felt uncomfortable at any time he should feel free to move to another topic or request that I switch the tape-recorder off. 'Fuchs' assured me that this would not be necessary: 'It doesn't bother me at all. You can ask me whatever you want' (A-6). Yet, despite these bold words 'Fuchs' often answered questions vaguely and frequently seemed to want to avoid certain issues.

'Fuchs' was born in the late 1930s. His father was not initially called up for service but was latterly ordered to join while he was trying to flee to the West with his family. His wife and two sons never heard from him again and presume that he died in a Soviet camp. 'Fuchs's' mother continued the journey West with the children. Chaos reigned at this time, and 'Fuchs' says that he remembers these traumatic events vividly, even though he was still so young, saying that those days 'sometimes seem like only yesterday' (A-6). The family was unable to carry on and began to return in the direction they had come. At first they found work on an estate in what is now Poland. Later they moved on to Soviet-occupied Germany, where 'Fuchs' began his schooling. He had missed a considerable amount of education and was the oldest in his class. He often organised activities with the younger pupils, and did so with such enthusiasm and aptitude that he was encouraged to go on to teacher training college. One day at college he caught sight of an announcement targeting young people from the East who might be interested in taking part in an exchange programme with students in Yugoslavia. 'Fuchs' and two friends followed up the advertisement and began to meet regularly with a woman in an office in West Berlin. They were asked about aspects of their educational training and were often given some money at the end of the meeting. These contacts carried on for about a year until the three friends noticed that they were being observed. They also felt that they were being given more and more concrete tasks to carry out by the woman and they had begun to realise that the promise of a holiday exchange had been merely a pretext. The three broke off the contact but noticed in the following months that they were still being observed: 'You learned how to spot that kind of thing, you know, really early on' (A-6). One day, shortly before their final exams, 'Fuchs' and his two friends were summoned to a meeting with Stasi officers and informed that they had not been involved with a youth organisation at all, but with a spy recruiting agency which had been on the verge of trying to engage them officially. 'Fuchs' says that after their statements had been taken they were told they would be allowed to sit their impending examinations, but that afterwards they would be required to do manual labour for a year. When, in 1993, 'Fuchs' was sacked as a result of his Stasi past he contested the sacking, stressing to me and in his letters to the Ministry of Justice that this 'victim-culprit' dichotomy should be considered when assessing his case.

The school where 'Fuchs' did eventually begin his teaching career had ties with the local prison. After new legislation granting prisoners educational opportunities was passed, he took up a post there. This was a welcome opportunity, as it meant that he would have Saturdays off and that he would earn more money. 'Fuchs' was put in charge of the teaching programme for inmates. In 1977 he was asked to work with the Stasi as an FIM and as such had about five or six prisoners reporting to him at any one time. When 'Fuchs' left the prison in the mid-1980s and took up another job, he was re-registered as an IMS.

'WOLFGANG'

'Wolfgang' stated emphatically at the beginning of our conversation that he considered it vital that he gave a lot of detailed information about his biography and about his belief in the principles of the GDR in order that his story be fully understood. His loyalty to the GDR was a recurring theme, and he became periodically quite animated when talking enthusiastically of certain positive aspects of life there and of how terrible things were by comparison under the current system.

'Wolfgang' was born in the midst of economic crisis in the late 1920s and was brought up in a small village in Saxony. His family was very poor and 'Wolfgang' was fortunate that the local teacher was keen to see someone from the village obtain a secondary education. He was the only working-class child at the school and was conscious of how poorly dressed he was in comparison to the other children there. 'Wolfgang' was called up in 1944 but never saw active service. Young men who had been born a year before him were involved in fighting in the latter days of the war, and many of them were killed in action. After finishing school, 'Wolfgang's' post as a civil servant involved having dealings with Soviet troops. During this time he made the acquaintance of many Russian officers with whom he says he had a good working relationship. Later he studied economics and took up a managerial post.

'Wolfgang' told me that he began work for the Stasi in the early 1960s. This work involved travelling undercover to West Berlin and meeting with a man there who gave him seemingly harmless pieces of information to pass back to his Stasi officer. The BStU was unable to uncover any material relating to 'Wolfgang'. It is possible that his file was destroyed in the extensive destruction of material from the foreign espionage department, the HVA, for which he may well have worked, or that the relevant material is still to be catalogued.

'STEPHANA'

'Stephana' was an intriguing and complex person. Before our first meeting I had the feeling that she did not actually want to go through with the arrangement at all, since arranging a time and date seemed to be an unnecessarily lengthy and complicated process. During our conversation, however, she was extremely co-operative and answered any questions thoughtfully and thoroughly. She seemed to have a real need to analyse her past. I spoke to her several times on the phone afterwards and visited her again that summer after viewing her file. The reasons for 'Stephana's' burning interest in contemplating her past are perhaps partly explained by the fact that she is someone who has spent many years becoming intensely involved with a variety of spiritual groups and tends to engage in much self-reflection. Her biography is also one which is characterised by periods of emotional disharmony and vulnerability. Her active interest in different ideological systems, in addition to an apparent need for stability, are perhaps partly responsible for the fact that someone who had not been at all sympathetic towards the State could become so bound to the Stasi after having been recruited as an informer only under considerable duress.

'Stephana' was born into a Catholic family in the 1960s. Theirs was one of few Catholic families in the area. She says that as a result she feels that she grew up in a Diaspora and emphasises that hers was a life characterised by inner and outer conflict. She did well at school, but difficulties arose when, because of her beliefs, she did not take part in the *Jugendweihe* ceremony, the ritual celebration of entrance into early adulthood which was commonly practised in the GDR. As a result 'Stephana' says that she was not allowed to complete her school leaving certificate and trained instead as a construction worker. 'Stephana' found this work frustrating because she felt that she was getting nowhere, and also because she had married someone who was doing well in a more stimulating job and who was disappointed that she had taken on, as he saw it, such menial work. She decided to take up work with the Post Office since this job also offered good childcare facilities at the time. The marriage still did not fare well, and they separated when 'Stephana' was twenty. The child remained in the custody of her ex-husband. 'Stephana' met someone else, had a second child and changed job again. Prior to being recruited as an informer, 'Stephana' had applied on two occasions to leave the GDR, once to marry an Algerian, and once to pursue her religious interests in a Buddhist centre in the West. She then began a new relationship and changed her mind about trying to go West.

In May 1985, 'Stephana' was picked up and interrogated by the Stasi. She had remained in contact with a former colleague with whom she had at one time discussed leaving the GDR. This man still intended to do so and had told her of his plan to escape by entering the American embassy and seeking asylum. He had requested that if he did not reappear within two days of his planned entry of the embassy she phone a number in West Berlin he gave her and relate the story to the person who answered. After the man did not return within the agreed time 'Stephana' complied with his request and phoned the number, which turned out to be that of a newspaper editorial office. The Stasi interrogated her about her role in this attempted escape and threatened her with legal action. She was then given the option of agreeing to work as an informer or of facing legal repercussions for her actions. She signed an oath of silence and, approximately four months later, on 1 October 1985, a declaration of commitment, so beginning a liaison with the Stasi which lasted until 1989.

Today 'Stephana' is still involved in various spiritual groups and has started up a small business.

'KATRIN'

'Katrin', alias Kerstin Kaiser-Nicht, was the only former unofficial employee with whom I spoke who was publicly known. She gained a seat in the German parliament in 1994 but, shortly after arriving in Bonn to take up this position, was put under pressure from her own party to resign, since it was felt that her Stasi past was damaging the PDS's public profile. Although she had made her Stasi past known before standing for election, she was accused of having disguised the true extent of these contacts (see I-19, 31, 50, 64).

'Katrin' was born in 1960. She enjoyed a happy childhood and, since she lived in a small town, claims that her only contact to the West was when an aunt of whom she was not particularly fond occasionally visited her family. As the daughter of two SED members, 'Katrin' was encouraged not just to be a member of, but to be active in the *Pioneers* and the *Free*

German Youth. She also played in a music group, and as a high achiever and popular student, fulfilled all the prerequisites to be among a group of students chosen to carry out their studies in Leningrad. While she was being prepared for these studies 'Katrin' was approached by the Stasi and asked to work for them. She agreed, and this relationship continued until she left Leningrad at the end of her studies in 1984.

'SONNENBLUME'

I contacted 'Sonnenblume' after reading her autobiography (J-110). 'Sonnenblume' contracted polio in 1940 when she was ten years old, and has been confined to a wheelchair ever since. Her mother was a teacher, who, she says, was suspended after being overheard saying that her daughter probably contracted her crippling disease after playing in a station where Russian soldiers had spat on the ground. Her father returned from the war in 1946 and found employment in a bank. 'Sonnenblume' had two brothers and one sister and describes her early childhood positively, despite the hunger and the cold that the family had to endure at this time. She completed her school leaving certificate at a school for physically disabled children, and went on to obtain a distance learning degree in translation from Leipzig University, subsequently setting herself up as a freelance translator of French.

As a person with a handicap, 'Sonnenblume' was not subjected to the same travel restrictions as other East Germans and often used this relative freedom to visit friends who had left the GDR and lived in West Germany. In the course of these visits her friends asked her to secretly relay information to another friend who was trying to get out of the GDR. When she was arrested by the Stasi on her way home from a trip West in late 1979, 'Sonnenblume' was interrogated about her role in this attempted escape. She was threatened with legal action if she did not agree to work for the Stasi and, after being detained through the night, signed a declaration of commitment. Her work for the Stasi lasted just over a year. A change in the officer in charge of her case gave her the courage to make the break from the organisation.

After 1989, increased competition in the translation business meant that 'Sonnenblume' was unable to continue to find work. She did, however, manage to translate one book about the life of a French singer after this time, something she considers a great personal success, since getting this contract involved a great deal of hard work and initiative. When her autobiography was published in 1993, 'Sonnenblume' was dismayed to find that several friends, including and above all the couple whom she had always visited in the West, broke off contact with her. She claims that she had told these friends of her Stasi contacts all those years ago, albeit in rather vague terms. She now feels hurt and disappointed that they have terminated the friendship. Other reactions to her book have been mixed, from horror and disgust that she should write as openly as she has done about details of her personal life, to statements of open admiration for having the courage to do so.

2

THE RECRUITMENT PROCESS

A work of art

> Recruitment cannot be carried out in an abstract and formal manner, but must be regarded almost like a work of art, which one must constantly strive to improve (J-62, p. 171).

The Stasi was not interested in recruiting individuals who voluntarily offered their services as informers. Instead, officers approached and actively recruited those who had been selected to be unofficial employees, so-called 'candidates'. A considerable amount of detailed planning went into the individual stages of recruitment. Once candidates had been found who corresponded to a particular Requirement Profile, both they and their immediate family were thoroughly screened. The recruitment process could take months, or even years. When suspicions that 'Rolf' was involved in foreign espionage were not confirmed it was decided, in 1983, to change his status from an OPK to a candidate (C-1a, p. 3). 'Rolf' remained a candidate for a further three years, until, in 1986, he was finally recruited as an unofficial employee (ibid. pp. 277–80). By this time 'Rolf's' history with the Stasi had encompassed a period of thirteen years. He had first come to their attention in 1973 when the informer 'Bernd Avis' had reported on 'Rolf's' connections to the West (C-1a, p. 57). Not all recruitments spanned such an extensive period of time. Some were achieved rapidly and without the investment of much effort on the part of the Stasi officer concerned. Yet, even in these cases, recruiting officers had to ensure that the timing and structure of the procedure's key components had been carefully planned in order to achieve maximum success.

After the preliminary stages of recruitment had been completed, that is the creation of a Requirement Profile and the selection and screening of a candidate, the recruiting officer faced the task of making contact with the individual concerned. As with any other aspect of the work concerning unofficial employees, the initial approach had to be carried out with utmost discretion. It was suggested that officers could ensure that their first contact to the candidate remain as discreet as possible by:

> Arranging that the candidate come and see the recruiting officer under a pretext
> Approaching the candidate directly
> Creating a situation which results in the candidate himself contacting the MfS.
> The contact meeting is to be carried out tactfully, and the personality and reactions of the candidate should be taken into consideration at all times (J-62, p. 344).

A Stasi survey carried out in 1973, analysing strategies of taking up contact with candidates, found that they were directly approached by a Stasi employee, usually at work or at home, in 34 per cent of cases considered (D-4, I, p. 294). Contact was initiated by written appointment in 33 per cent of all cases, by telephone in 17 per cent, and by an approach through a third party in the remaining 16 per cent (ibid.). In the majority of recruitments the initial contact with the candidate thus had an official character. The formal tone of the preliminary contact resulted in candidates feeling more duty-bound to appear for the first meeting and, furthermore, often meant that their suspicions were not aroused. Recruiting officers were concerned to avoid a situation where candidates prematurely came to the conclusion that they were to be recruited to work with the Stasi. If this were to happen, it might allow a candidate who was negatively disposed to the idea of such work time to plan a possible defence strategy and perhaps to inform others of the forthcoming meeting, so limiting the chances of a fruitful working relationship. In order that the candidate did not suspect the true purpose of the summons, the Stasi often resorted to its much-loved tactic of employing a legend, described in the Stasi dictionary as a 'plausible pretence used to mislead people about the MfS's true goals and intentions' (F-3, p. 240). In the study mentioned, the majority of those who received a written invitation to the contact meeting were sent a police summons. The remaining candidates were led to believe that they would be meeting with representatives of various other state organs, but never explicitly the Stasi (D-4, I, p. 294). Even when the potential informers were aware that they were to meet with a representative from the Stasi, they were generally misled as to the true purpose of this meeting. The authors of the study suggest that a legend could be so constructed to convey to candidates the feeling that they were regarded as someone to whom confidential information could be entrusted. One possible legend would therefore be to lead the candidate to believe that the Stasi was interested in enlisting them to help investigate reports that a child in their immediate neighbourhood had been abused: 'The deep emotional effect of being told something like this is of advantage to both parties. The candidate believes that this is the true reason for the meeting and feels that the MfS has placed trust in him' (D-4, II, p. 417).

It was essential that the time lag between the notification of the meeting and the event itself was optimal for the specific situation and candidate. If the time lapse were too great, the chances that the candidate would inform someone of the planned meeting increased. One potential unofficial employee is quoted describing the disturbing half hour he spent between being called to a meeting with a Stasi officer and the imminent appointment. In this time he contemplated the different stages of his public life, searching for potential misdemeanours which might have resulted in this unexpected summons: 'This inner tension did not leave me until the beginning of the meeting' (D-4, I, pp. 301–2). There was an obvious danger that in a case like this the candidate would, through increasing uneasiness and nervousness, be unable to remain silent about the approaching meeting. Yet, the inducement of this cognitive state could also work to the recruiting officers' advantage. The relief on the part of the candidates to discover that they were not to be rebuked for having done something wrong, but had rather been selected to assume a position of trust, may have been significant in their decision to agree to work as an informer. The desire of candidates or newly recruited informers to diminish their fears of the unknown by complying with the MfS could be exploited at various stages in the recruitment process. Both 'Stephana' and 'Sonnenblume', for example, describe the period immediately after their initial meeting with Stasi officers as an emotionally turbulent one, during which they were plagued by doubts and fears (A-8, A-10). After the two women had been contacted by the officers in charge of their cases and the work for the Stasi had begun to take on concrete form, they experienced intense relief that this period of uncertainty had passed. 'Stephana' and 'Sonnenblume' were consequently less negatively disposed towards the notion of working with the Stasi, since such co-operation seemed to offer a more satisfactory alternative to waiting and uncertainty.

After the contact meeting had taken place and candidates had been made aware of the true reason as to why they had been summoned, it was necessary to ensure that this fact remain secret. To this end, further legends were created. After, as a result of her detainment by the Stasi, 'Sonnenblume' returned home a day later than expected from her trip to

West Germany, she was instructed to explain to her father that she had been delayed because of a formality concerning her passport (C-8a, p. 70). Similarly, although in his case the period of absence was relatively brief, it was considered necessary to create a legend to explain why 'Theodor' had left the office when he was summoned to his contact meeting. Accordingly, he was asked to bring a piece of equipment with him which he had previously borrowed from a man whose office was located near the meeting room. Returning the item thus served as the pretext for 'Theodor's' absence (C-2a, I, p. 141).

Despite all this intensive planning, it could not be expected that a candidate would agree 'spontaneously and unquestioningly' to agree to work for the Stasi (D-9, p. 35). In most cases, some enticement and coaching was required. At this crucial early stage, however, it was important that the candidate did make some kind of commitment. This was a delicate matter, and in the late 1950s and early 1960s concern arose that a number of those who had been asked to work as informers had left to go to the West shortly afterwards (E-1, pp. 42–6). It was felt that those who had left were individuals who, before being approached by the Stasi, would not have been likely to leave the GDR. Stasi officers were thus to be discouraged from trying to recruit too many informers too quickly. All too often, this report continued, compromising material was being used to coerce candidates into signing an agreement, with the result that they felt themselves 'cornered to such an extent, that they see escape as the only way out' (E-1, p. 43). It was suggested therefore that more effort be made to convince candidates of the political necessity of the task at hand, instead of pressurising them into agreement. That sufficient time was not being invested to this end was seen to be reflected in the fact that:

> As long as the unofficial employees are being asked to write reports of a *general* nature, they work. As soon as they are asked to give concrete reports on a specific person, however, they take flight. This means that these people are not being adequately prepared for their actual tasks or convinced of their political necessity (E-1, p. 43).

Stasi officers were thus tending to encourage their informers to formally commit themselves at a premature stage and subsequently demanding that they compile reports on specific individuals before sufficient persuasive tactics had been employed. The recruitment of informers for the long-term required that one kept sight of the fact that, although written commitment was desired in the majority of cases, 'positive co-operation on the part of the unofficial employee is decisive, not the statement of commitment' (F-5, I, p. 83). Insisting upon written confirmation of the agreement when the candidate seemed unwilling to take this step could only endanger the situation (J-62, p. 174). It was thus often the case that generally compliant candidates were not as likely to be asked to make a written commitment as those who were less enamoured with the idea of working for the Stasi. The case of the physicist Robert Havemann provides one such example. In the late 1960s and 1970s Havemann became one of the Stasi's most despised dissidents in the GDR and suffered the gross injustices which accompanied this status until his death in 1982. In the early days of the new German Democratic Republic, however, Havemann, a convinced anti-fascist, was a strong supporter of the state and, under the cover name 'Leitz', was registered for seven years as a Secret Informer (an earlier term for an unofficial employee). When he was officially recruited in 1956, Havemann was not required to sign a written commitment: 'As a result of the fact that he has been active for us for some time and because of his social standing it was considered unnecessary to obtain a written commitment, since this would be a mere formality' (I-56, p. 87). In this early period, the writer Christa Wolf also agreed to co-operate with the Stasi and, at least initially, seemed prepared to deliver the kind of information required. When asked if she would be prepared to work for the Stasi, Wolf agreed 'without much hesitation' (J-99, p. 90). Wolf seemed uneasy, however, about making an oath of silence. At the mention of such secrecy she became visibly uncomfortable and as a result 'a written commitment was not insisted upon because of her state of mind' (ibid. p. 90).

Before being asked to sign the actual declaration of commitment candidates were often asked to make an oath of silence about the initial meeting or meetings. In effect the oath of silence had a dual purpose. It increased the likelihood that the candidate would remain silent about having been approached by the Stasi, and it was also a candidate's first commitment to becoming a fully-fledged unofficial employee. In the majority of cases the signing of the official commitment was, however, still fundamental to the recruitment process:

> The oath is more than just the verbal or written formulation of commitment, but also seals the complex mental process which the candidate has been going through (D-4, II, p. 662).
>
> In cases where the candidate is not wholly convinced about what he is doing, the effect of this action must be particularly exploited,

> since it strengthens the awareness of having taken on an obligation (ibid. II, pp. 664–5).

The above statements of theory certainly seem to have been borne out in practice in the case of 'Thaer'. 'Thaer' tells me that despite the doubts he experienced after having signed the declaration of commitment, he saw the matter as sealed once he had taken this step and consequently resigned himself to the fact (A-5).

Once candidates had committed themselves, the Stasi made efforts to ensure that the agreement was seen as binding. The wording of the written commitment, for example, sometimes referred to the repercussions the informer would suffer if the agreement were broken. The commitment was also further intensified by the fact that the newly-recruited unofficial employees were asked to assume a cover name for future contact. In some cases a name was suggested, in others the informer made the choice. Stasi researchers Korth, Jonak and Scharbert advised Stasi officers to present the idea of a cover name rather as a ' "second name", "working name" or "pseudonym" ' (D-4, II, p. 668). In line with this theory, on 17 November 1975, the newly-recruited 'Theodor' wrote in the text of his written commitment: 'I have chosen the name "Theodor" as a pseudonym' (C-2a, I, p. 11).

After recruitment, the new unofficial employee was theoretically to be assigned a task for completion before the first official meeting (J-62, pp. 349–50). Part of 'Theodor's' first duty was, for example, to complete a detailed report on a colleague of his which was to include the following information:

> professional and political development
> connections/travel activities
> hobbies/interests/passions
> specific behaviour patterns
> political attitude/any contradictions (C-2a, I, 143).

The strategies described here have covered the recruitment process and how aspects of it intensified the bond and commitment on the part of the informer to the Stasi. The motivation on the part of the candidate to actually agree to work for the Stasi will be considered in the following chapter.

3

ON MOTIVATION

According to the 1979 guidelines for work with unofficial employees, recruitment strategy could be based upon the candidates' positive political stance, on their personal needs and interests, on the desire to atone for misdemeanours, or on a combination of all three approaches (J-62, p. 347).

The first of these strategies is defined as follows:

> Recruitments based on the positive political stance of the candidate should build upon the candidate's outlook on life as well as on their moral and political convictions, thus developing their willingness to work with the MfS (ibid.).

Earlier guidelines from 1958 specify that this basis for recruitment was to be the most frequently employed (ibid. p. 212). A case study by Stasi researchers, Seidler and Schmidt, suggests that as many as 81 per cent of informers in Karl-Marx-Stadt had been recruited on the basis of political conviction (D-6, I, 6). Since this form of recruitment was supposed to be the most frequently employed, it is possible that the authors looked to find evidence that this was realised in practice. In addition, recruiting officers who were aware of the content of the guidelines may have tended to exaggerate the number of times when this was the case.

Several of those I spoke to were certainly keen to emphasise that their political convictions had been fundamental in motivating them to work with the Stasi. 'Wolfgang' wasted no time in making this point, beginning our conversation with a statement of his loyalty to the GDR which he was later to repeat and elaborate upon. Likewise, 'Katrin', born in 1960, argued: 'I had only ever known the Wall in my lifetime and my childhood on this side of it was pretty free of conflict' (A-9). Both these informers and many others claim that, when approached by the Stasi, it seemed to them to be 'the most normal thing in the world' to agree to co-operate as an unofficial employee (ibid.). It should be taken into consideration, when examining such claims of fervent conviction, that 'Katrin' and 'Wolfgang' may tend now to exaggerate somewhat the extent of their commitment to supporting the SED in order to justify their behaviour in the face of what has sometimes been harsh societal criticism. 'Katrin's' biographical details do, however, read rather like those of the almost archetypal patriotic GDR citizen, indicating a high level of sympathy or at least compliance with state ideology. Although she seems to have subsequently doubted her actions, it is easy to comprehend why she might, at least initially, have considered it self-explanatory to agree to work for the Stasi.

Some of those who seem to have been recruited primarily on the basis of a pre-existing positive stance towards the state stress now that they viewed working for the Stasi as an integral part of their working lives. 'Falke' says that, since in his role with the police force he had worked alongside Stasi officers anyway for six years, he did not have to think long before agreeing to be an informer (A-3). In a letter to the Ministry of Justice contesting his sacking on the grounds of having been an unofficial employee, 'Fuchs' argued similarly that, since Stasi officers were closely involved in the running of the prison, had he, a prison employee, refused to co-operate with them, he could only have imagined that there would be serious repercussions (B-6).

Recruiting informers such as those mentioned above tended to be a relatively straightforward task for the Stasi officers concerned. In accordance with the usual procedure, careful checks had to be made on the candidates and their immediate family, but once these had been carried out and the contact meeting been planned, it was fairly certain that the candidate would agree to the proposal without much further ado. If any uncertainty at all was detected on the part of such a basically willing candidate, it could generally be quickly put to rest, as was the case with 'Theodor':

> The candidate immediately declared his willingness to work with us but tried to impose some restrictions concerning personal details and information on people close to him. It was explained to him, however, that such a stance was contradictory to the nature of our work, which the candidate recognised and then immediately gave some information about himself and his family (C-2a, I, p. 141).

'Theodor' seems to have needed only to be given a very gentle assurance that what he was doing was officially sanctioned. Not all candidates came to the recruitment meeting with such pre-established political conviction, and in these cases the Stasi had thus to first convince them that there was a politically and morally justifiable purpose to agreeing to work for them. The writer Günter Kunert discusses how a plausible, meaningful and justifiable purpose to working for the Stasi was presented to informers (J-47, p. 18). This tactic was particularly useful in cases where it could not be taken for granted that the candidate would agree unhesitatingly to work for the Stasi: 'This final secular transcendence helped the informer to do his work, since he relinquished any individual responsibility for his actions. In this way scruples could be eliminated' (ibid.). Looking back, it seems that 'Rolf' was certainly swayed by the, in Kunert's terms, 'offer of a meaningful purpose' presented to him at the contact meeting. As a result of his active commitment to environmental issues, 'Rolf' had many contacts with individuals whose activities the Stasi was keen to closely monitor. The officers involved in 'Rolf's' recruitment were well informed of the candidate's critical and sceptical view of the GDR's policies on environmental protection. This information was used to construct a basis for recruitment which stressed the necessity of working together with the Stasi in order to bring about change in these environmental practices and, on a wider scale, to help ensure world peace, an issue which also concerned 'Rolf'. During the contact meeting, 'Rolf' expressed his view that not enough was being undertaken to combat pollution in the GDR (C-1a, p. 277). 'Rolf' was therefore critical of government policies, but did not reject the state as such, still believing that change was possible. The Stasi officers cleverly managed to turn this critical stance, combined with 'Rolf's' ultimate faith in the state, into an offer of a meaningful purpose to working for the Stasi, an offer this candidate had difficulty refusing:

> I used to read the *Weltbühne* newspaper at that time and once there was an article in it and yes, it sounds mad, but it said that it was important at that time to do more than just get on with your daily life, that you should do more than just get up and go to work if you wanted to ensure peace, do something so that things didn't just go on as they had done, and . . . but the jump from that . . . Yes, I have to say that at that moment I wasn't unwilling. I was almost convinced that it was a good thing, that it would help prevent something (A-1).

Initially, 'Rolf' was led to believe that he would be involved in preventing military espionage and given the impression that the Stasi was concerned about any environmental pollution he told them of. Although somewhat hesitant, he decided that he could justify such an undertaking:

> In a word they made use of my, yeah what should I say, my love of peace, maybe that sounds a bit mushy, my concerns for the world, and they said: 'You can help us to fight this together.' Yes, and then I said: ' I've got nothing against that' (A-1).

'Rolf' committed himself in writing, and the motivation for recruitment was consequently noted in his Personal File as: 'Positive moral conviction, in particular concerning sustaining peace, disarmament in the socialist states and promoting the protection of nature and the environment' (C-1a, p. 38).

In some cases the sense that there was an honourable purpose involved in working for the Stasi was short-lived and functioned only as a motivating factor at the time of recruitment. 'Rolf', for example, soon realised that the Stasi was not concerned with environmental issues and that he was to be increasingly encouraged to give information about people within his circle of acquaintances. It became more and more difficult for him to justify to himself why he was working for the Stasi, and he eventually broke off the contact.

Other unofficial employees who remained active often endeavoured to keep alive the belief in the purpose of what they were doing. They were not alone in this endeavour, since the Stasi was equally keen to continue convincing them that their actions were morally and politically justifiable. Much emphasis was placed on training the informers to this way of thinking. The 1958 guidelines stipulate that the political education of informers is the most important principle of the work with them, and further: 'The commitment of the unofficial employee has to be developed to such an extent that he would even be prepared to give his life for the cause' (J-62, pp. 212, 219). However, in spite of the obvious attempts of the Stasi officers to educate and develop their unofficial employees to this way of thinking, many became sceptical and disillusioned. One informer describes the battle of trying to maintain the belief in the good of what he was doing as follows:

> There was always this broken morality, it's for a good cause – order and security – and we have to protect the country, it all sounds fair enough . . . until you think about the fact that you're involved in something that when it comes down to it isn't politically or morally justifiable (J-71, p. 149).

* * *

For those potential informers who were not particularly pre-disposed to the idea of supporting the state and the collective, the recruitment strategy was structured so as to appeal more to their personal needs and interests. The guidelines for the work with informers subdivide this strategy for recruitment into material needs, social needs and intellectual interests (J-62, p. 348).

Material needs are defined as those, 'which are to do with acquiring financial rewards or other advantages, with being relieved of material burdens and duties, with maintaining a particular lifestyle' (J-62, p. 348). This definition should not be taken to mean that a significant number of informers received a salary for their services. This was really only the case for a small minority of regular informers and for the full-time unofficial employees. The Stasi aimed to develop a sense of loyalty and obligation rather than to create a business partnership with its informers. The political tuning of the employees was therefore to be achieved through 'a clever balance of praise and recognition as well as critical feedback' (ibid. p. 324). Stasi researchers, Korth, Jonak and Scharbert, conclude that candidate P.'s decision to agree to co-operate was positively influenced by the help she received in securing her child a place in a psychiatric clinic (D-4, II, p. 618). The authors view this kind of enticement positively, clearly distinguishing it from other less desirable motives:

> Those material interests which represent commercially based thinking, the egoistic striving for advantage, are to be judged quite differently. [. . .] A stable motivational framework cannot be built upon such egoistic needs, since they must be constantly fed by ever new rewards (D-4, II, p. 619).

If, at the recruitment meeting, the Stasi officers promised or hinted at the advantages to be gained from working for them, then these tended to be of the kind from which 'candidate P.' benefited, rather than financial rewards. After they began working, many informers did, however, receive regular financial bonuses and presents. 'Sonnenblume', for example, was presented with champagne and flowers on the occasion of International Women's Day in 1978. Her Stasi officer noted afterwards that she seemed genuinely pleased to receive these gifts (C-8b, p. 43).

In conclusion, although the material recognition which unofficial employees received may have strengthened the desire to continue working for the Stasi, in the majority of cases it cannot be seen as having been a major motivational factor at the time of recruitment.

The second subgroup, 'social needs', are defined as those, 'which are to do with acquiring a particular standing and reputation, with being trusted and highly regarded in society, with compensating for real or apparent handicaps' (J-62, p. 348). It is important at this point to consider that prospective informers could not simply approach the Stasi and offer their services. In fact the guidelines from 1952 warn: 'Particular care should be taken with those individuals who voluntarily offer their services' (ibid. p. 173). Candidates had been carefully selected for the task and this was made clear to them. The effort which was invested throughout recruitment and during the working relationship to ensure that they felt at ease could have a flattering effect, and perhaps gave some candidates the impression that such recruitments were not everyday occurrences. Guidelines from the 1950s suggest that the informers should be made to feel comfortable by being received in a clean and tidy flat and by being offered a little something to eat or drink, and furthermore: 'One should not forget to offer female unofficial employees something sweet to eat' (ibid. p. 189).

'Intellectual interests', the final subgroup in the category of personal needs and interests, are defined as those, 'which are to do with new and different activities and areas of operation, with a change in the pattern of daily life, with being confronted with previously unknown problems and experiences' (ibid. p. 348).

Much of the daily life of an informer was undoubtedly staggeringly banal, and the majority of informers were themselves 'the complete opposite of James Bond, practically the mirror image of Mr and Mrs Joe Bloggs' (J-55, p. 42). Yet this is not to say that the thrill of feeling just a little bit like an exotic spy was not sometimes influential in a candidate's decision to agree to work for the Stasi. The secrecy and intrigue involved in even just the arrangement of the contact or recruitment meetings was certainly enough to stimulate a sense of adventure in some candidates. The frequently ensuing banality and routine of the work could not be foreseen at this time. 'Thaer' recounted the decidedly adventurous story of the way in which he was recruited as follows (A-5). As he was travelling home through East Germany to West Germany one day, 'Thaer' became involved in what he took to be a casual conversation with an East German guard. After chatting to him for some time, the guard offered to set up a meeting between 'Thaer' and an acquaintance of his, with a view to giving 'Thaer', who had studied agriculture, the opportunity of visiting a collective smallholding. The meeting became the first in a series of trips by 'Thaer' to the GDR, during which he and the border-guard's 'friend' talked of many things, including the possibility of setting up a youth exchange programme between the two Germanys. 'Thaer' experienced his trips to the East as stimulating and exciting. He also began to regard his East German escort as a friend. Finally, when the question was put to him on the morning after the two men had spent a merry evening together at the Leipzig trade fair, 'Thaer' agreed without much hesitation to work for the Stasi.

If not quite as prolonged and complex as that of 'Thaer', the recruitment of an informer within East Germany could be equally exciting. By use of a legend, 'Theodor' was summoned to his recruitment on the 14 November 1975. The recruitment ran smoothly, and it was agreed that whenever 'Theodor' or his Stasi officer wished to contact one another they should incorporate a code phrase into a fitting context within a written or oral communication (C-2a, I, 142). The use of such code-words or -phrases was common and perhaps helped to stimulate a sense of adventure in some candidates. Both 'Thaer' and 'Theodor' would, for different reasons, probably have agreed without much further ado to work for the Stasi. The excitement associated with recruitment, and the anticipation of future mental stimulation, was more of an added bonus rather than the principal motivational force.

* * *

In general, it was not considered correct procedure to use coercion as a means of recruiting informers. Seidler and Schmidt found that only 7.7 per cent of the informers in their study were recorded as having been recruited using 'compromising material' (D-6, I, p. 6). Once again, it is difficult to know to what extent this figure gives a true representation, given that both the authors of the study and/or the Stasi officers may have underplayed their use of this method in light of the fact that the 1958 guidelines specified that this basis for recruitment was only to be used when other possibilities were not available (J-62, p. 213). The 1979 guidelines did not state this explicitly, but did caution that if recruitment was to be made on the basis of desire to atone for misdemeanours, approval had to be sought in advance from superiors (ibid. p. 349).

The key element to this type of recruitment was clearly the existence of suitable compromising material. In the case of 'Sonnenblume', this took the form of the evidence that she had played a role in the attempt of a woman to escape from the GDR. Her task had been to relay messages to the woman from mutual friends in West Germany. 'Sonnenblume' was arrested by the Stasi as she was returning from a visit to the West, taken to a nearby police station and questioned through the night about this 'courier service' (C-8a, p. 67). One of the recruiting officers had predicted before the meeting: 'It is to be expected that after a sense of guilt has been awakened in the candidate she will declare herself willing to work for the MfS' (ibid.). The next morning 'Sonnenblume' did, indeed, sign a written commitment in which she pledged 'to support the Ministry for State Security as much as I can by helping to clarify problems and fulfilling duties in order to make up for my actions' (ibid. p. 63). It was not clear to her at this point what form this contact to the Stasi would take and 'Sonnenblume' describes the following days and nights before the first meeting with her Stasi officer as extremely distressing. She did not know what lay before her: 'That's why I was caught in this terrible uncertainty about what was going to happen next, when they said: "You'll be hearing from us"' (A-10).

The pattern of 'Stephana's' recruitment bears strong similarities to that of 'Sonnenblume's'. 'Stephana' was picked up from her home on 22 May 1985 and questioned about her role in the attempted escape from the GDR of a friend of hers. At the end of the interrogation, she signed an initial commitment to the Stasi, which was worded as follows: 'In order to avoid further legal action being taken against me, I hereby agree to work for the MfS to make up for my actions' (C-6a, p. 7). 'Stephana' was subsequently sent home and she, too, experienced the subsequent period of uncertainty as highly distressing. She says that she suffered from a sort of paranoia, unable to shake off the feeling that she was being constantly observed and followed (A-8). Regular meetings soon began to be set up between 'Stephana' and Stasi officers, during which she was asked to give information on the various religious groups with which she was involved. Just over four months after the initial interrogation, 'Stephana' signed the official commitment and was to remain active as an informer until the Stasi's demise in late 1989.

Both 'Stephana' and 'Sonnenblume' were certainly coerced into agreeing to work for the Stasi to some extent. Psychologist Hans-Joachim Maaz argues, however, that if people had really been forced to work for the Stasi, these individuals would have come forward after 1989 and denounced those who had made them do so. The fact that this did not happen is an indication, according to Maaz, that a certain willingness on the part of the person being blackmailed should always be taken into account in these matters (J-55, p. 87).

Evidence does seem to suggest that refusing to agree to work for the Stasi rarely led to any negative repercussions for the person concerned. Yet, since this was something which one could only establish after the fact, refusing to work for the Stasi did require a certain amount of courage and potential risk. Martin Schubert managed to dissuade the Stasi officers trying to recruit him by insisting that his wife join them in their meeting and by claiming that he could never keep a secret. His wife backed up his claim. The men went away and Schubert reflects:

> In retrospect it seems strange to me that they accepted this. They didn't come back but left us in peace. I was amazed about it because for a long time I was worried that something would happen (J-41, p. 356).

Further examples of such resistance are given by Andreas Schmidt, who documents how one man was able to escape the Stasi's clutch simply by telling the recruiting officers who approached him that he was not the 'informer type' (J-80, p. 169). Another man rarely turned up for meetings and only reported positively about others when present (ibid. p. 171). Such behaviour was referred to as 'avoidance and deception manoeuvres' and, when it was detected, the Stasi quickly lost interest in the candidate or newly-recruited informer (ibid. p. 174).

The Stasi was keen to recruit informers within a positive motivational framework. This served internal ideology and, if successful, meant that the informers were more likely to be reliable. Even in cases where the candidate was to be coerced into agreeing to comply, the guidelines for recruitment emphasise the positive aspect of such co-operation, that is the atonement. A sense of guilt was to be aroused in candidates in order that they felt the need to make good their misdemeanours. There was no room in this terminology for negative concepts such as recruitment on the basis of fear. That is not to say that fear was not at times instrumental in a candidate's decision to agree to work as an informer. The Stasi's ideological structures did not, however, allow fear to be documented and thus sanctioned as a motivational factor. Inducing fear was certainly used as a means of manipulating candidates, but this method was rarely noted in the reports relating to recruitment.

The informer was to be an ally in the fight against the enemy, and it was the task of the Stasi officers to educate the candidate or newly-recruited informers and so aim to create a meaningful purpose for an individual who was initially negatively disposed. The documents relating to 'Stephana's' recruitment state that she placed emphasis on including the word 'continue' in her final written statement of commitment, which read: 'I hereby agree to continue to work for the MfS and have chosen 'Stephana' as my cover name' (C-6a, pp. 39, 7). 'Stephana' was clearly keen to understand the future contact with the Stasi as a continuation of what had gone before in the months leading up to the official recruitment.

In other words, it seems to have been important to her to emphasise that her compliance was a direct consequence of her interrogation and the threats made against her. On the other side, although coercion was used initially, the officers she was working under were interested in altering this premise by educating 'Stephana' on the 'moral justification' of aiding the fight against the enemy (D-5, p. 47):

> Nurturing the correct feelings towards the enemy strengthens the unofficial employees' conviction that what they are doing is right and that they are superior to the enemy, and must result in them having contempt and loathing for him. A strong desire to actively take on the enemy results from such passionate convictions, as well as a greater sense of duty and selfless commitment (Mielke, F-5, II, p. 532).

This MfS theory could never be a reality. The informer network, if it were to be effective, depended on informers having close, even intimate contacts to the 'enemy'. A good informer was a friend and neighbour to an individual whom the Stasi had placed under observation. The motivation behind working for the Stasi was rarely hatred of the designated enemy. Such an explanation of motivation agreed, however, with Stasi ideology and therefore found its place in the guidelines relating to the recruitment and subsequent political education of unofficial employees.

In the months following the signing of the official commitment, the nature of the co-operation between 'Stephana' and the Stasi began to take on a new form. She was given more precise goal-oriented tasks and asked to report on specific individuals. By complying with these tasks, 'Stephana' slipped increasingly into the web of deceit and intrigue which was part of the daily life of an informer, with the result that fear was no longer as significant a factor in motivating her actions. It may be partly for this reason that, after 1989, former unofficial employees did not denounce the Stasi officers they worked for. At the time when they agreed to work for the Stasi, fear may well have been a strong motivational factor, but as the contact continued, this was decreasingly the case. The Stasi worked hard to convince the newly-recruited informers of the honourable nature of their actions and the informers themselves often managed to rationalise the situation, thus suppressing any nagging doubts about the morally questionable compromises they were making.

A further significant motivational basis which is not documented in the guidelines may simply have been the passivity factor, which is that, at the moment when the proposal was put to a candidate, the easiest option was simply to agree. The Stasi's policy of carefully selecting and screening potential informers meant that becoming an unofficial employee was not the result of decisive action, but was rather the path of least resistance. The Stasi files are testimony to the fact that some potential informers did withstand attempts to recruit them, leading the writer Lutz Rathenow to describe these documents as 'a monument to resistance, a chronology of civilian courage in the GDR' (J-68, p. 1466). The majority of those approached did not, however, find the courage to which Rathenow refers. 'Wolfgang', for example, claimed that he 'could just never say no' (A-7). 'Sonnenblume' likewise defends her compliance by arguing that she was 'not made to be a hero' and always preferred 'a compromise' (A-10). The inability to say no was significant in many cases. This passivity factor in motivation was one which the Stasi's recruiting officers must have been aware of through their dealings with candidates, but which, because of its negative nature, did not fit with internal ideology and is thus not to be found in the guidelines.

It is not always easy to obtain objective statements from informers concerning their motivation for agreeing to work for the Stasi. An analysis of the statements they do make in conjunction with the files held on these individuals does, however, facilitate our understanding of the mechanisms at work. For many candidates, it was the interplay of several of the various motivating factors discussed above which swayed their decision to agree to cooperate. This motivational basis did not necessarily remain constant throughout the course of their work for the Stasi. On the subject of motivation, Walter Schilling argued: 'The motives at play are not sufficient justification for having worked as an informer' (F-13, p. 94). The motives at recruitment may, indeed, not be sufficient justification for an individual's subsequent actions as an informer. In any confrontation with this aspect of the Stasi legacy it is, however, vital to understand the methodological and cognitive mechanisms which were involved in such a recruitment, both from the point of view of the Stasi and from that of the informer.

4

BETWEEN THEORY AND PRACTICE

A day in the life of a Stasi informer

The essential task of the Stasi's army of informers was to deliver information which would allow plans to be constructed to destroy or neutralise the enemy. Such information was classified as being of operational significance and defined as follows:

> Information about events, actions, people, establishments, objects and the relationships between them, which allows measures to be taken against existing or anticipated security threats, and which can therefore be used to help determine and realise concrete politically operative measures (F-3, p. 171).

In order to obtain this kind of information, Stasi officers were instructed to thoroughly plan all meetings with informers, and to record the details of the preparation and of the meeting itself in the standard Meeting Report form (J-62, pp. 179–85). Meetings were to take place in locations specified for this purpose. If, in an exceptional case, a meeting was planned outside these designated areas, clearance from above was theoretically to be obtained (ibid. p. 333).

Each meeting with an unofficial employee was to have three key components. Officers were to lead a conversation with the unofficial employee about personal matters, to obtain a report from them, and then to inform and instruct them about their next task (ibid. p. 223). Training was given on how to most effectively carry out the meetings. Officers would, for example, be played a tape of a meeting and asked to evaluate the significance of the information which the informer gave (D-11). The trainees were then asked to decide on a possible next assignment for the informer, taking into account that the format of the meetings was not to become routine and predictable if it could be avoided at all (J-62, p. 180; D-11, p. 8).

The reality of the daily work with informers did not always correspond to the above theory. Officers who met with the same unofficial employee on a regular basis over a period of many years were bound to find it increasingly difficult to prevent the format of these meetings becoming routine. That meetings often did begin to follow a set pattern is reflected in the reports. On numerous occasions, the wording of the notes relating to the preparation and execution of the meetings with 'Falke' is, for example, either very similar or even exactly the same (C-3b, II, pp. 7–8, 26–7, 83–4). 'Falke' was usually asked to give a character description of a colleague or describe reactions among colleagues to a particular event. Sometimes the information which he gave was judged as being of operational significance; often, however, it was not. Evidence suggests that at any given time the majority of unofficial employees were not actively involved in working on specific cases. Seidler and Schmidt found that 77.6 per cent of informers they included in their study were neither active in cases running or in preparation and furthermore, that as many as 24.2 per cent had never been involved with such work (D-6, I, p. 183).

The Stasi's network of informers was thus in many ways chaotically and inefficiently managed. In 1971, checks showed that for quite some time no meetings had been held with up to 30 per cent of informers who were registered active (F-5, I, p. 295). This situation may have arisen partly because of the uneven distribution of informers amongst Stasi officers. Young colleagues tended to be given a disproportionately high workload, with some having a network of up to thirty unofficial employees in their care, while departmental heads often had no caseload at all (F-5, I, pp. 292, 299). It is likely that these young officers were swamped by the vast administrative commitment which each case required, and were at times unable to meet demands adequately. Perhaps this partly accounts for the fact that standard administrative procedure was not always strictly observed. Documents in the files are often not in chronological order, and much material is inefficiently duplicated several times by hand. Reports of meetings were often written up several days after the event, although they were in theory to be completed within twenty-four hours (J-62, p. 224). The sheer volume of paperwork involved in any one case meant that those who were in charge of up to thirty informers were under considerable pressure and possibly did not find the time to consider how their informers could be put to more effective use in working on specific cases.

Many of these young Stasi officers may also have been insufficiently familiar with some of the most basic principles of the work with unofficial employees. Pedagogic material compiled for the JHS warned that deficiencies in the system resulted partly from the fact that officers were not recognising information as being of significance and were thus unable to fully exploit the potential of the unofficial employees (D-10, pp. 14–15). One study found that 110 of 260 informers who had been told their services were no longer required on the grounds that the contacts were no longer fruitful actually had contacts to individuals whom the Stasi had identified as 'interesting' (D-7, I, p. 13).

It was completely within the realms of possibility that in their time with the Stasi unofficial employees might never deliver information which was judged to be useful. When 'Sonnenblume' broke off her contact to the Stasi, for example, the officer in charge of her case reported being not particularly sorry to see her go since he felt that she had never supplied him with useful information (C-8a, p. 149). The Stasi was not interested in maintaining contact to those who could not supply them with the kind of information they needed, and for this reason contact to 'Theodor' was brought to an end in 1985, when it was felt he was no longer supplying the right type of information (C-2a, II, 181). If it was often the case that the officers did not recognise information as being significant, then it is, of course, possible that both 'Sonnenblume' and 'Theodor' were actually delivering potentially useful reports and that it would have been in the Stasi's interests to maintain contact to them. Conversely, informers who really were of no use to the Stasi were often kept on the records in order to boost overall numbers. Some officers may thus have tended to over- rather than undervalue the significance of information they received. 'Thaer' certainly felt that more fuss was made of him and the information he gave than was really warranted (A-5). This may well have been the case, yet 'Thaer' could not know where, when, or in what manner the apparently banal reports he gave were used by the Stasi. Indeed, many of the reports on specific individuals to be found in the Stasi files are concerned with apparently trivial information. A key issue is also the question of whether the individual under surveillance led a well-ordered family life. It was, however, precisely this sort of seemingly trivial and banal personal information which could be extremely useful to the Stasi. Such information could potentially be used to blackmail others, and it also helped construct a comprehensive personality profile of designated state enemies, which would facilitate the creation of plans to dispose of them. Other apparently banal personal information also often found application. Reports, for example, that Gerd and Ulrike Poppe's marriage was going through a rough patch led to the planning of measures to deepen this rift, among other things by setting a male informer on Ulrike, whose task it was to seduce her (I-37).

The Stasi was interested in the private affairs not only of those who it sought to destroy, but also of its own people. 'Theodor', who was requested to get his family life in order when it was discovered that his wife was having an affair with a work colleague of his, compared the morality of the Stasi in the 1960s and 1970s to that of the Catholic Church (A-2). 'Falke's' private life was also a subject of concern to his Stasi officer, and he was told that he ought to re-marry his ex-wife, with whom he had rekindled his relationship (C-3a, p. 212). The often rather absurd attempts to maintain a factual objectivity when documenting such incidents is evident in one of the reports written by 'Falke's' Stasi officer, who noted: 'In answer to the questions regarding personal affairs and problems, the source expressed no concerns in this area. To the question regarding relationships with women the source answered in the negative' (C-3b, II, p. 94).

Much of the other material contained in the files seems at first glance equally trivial. There are many sketches of people's flats to be found, some of which come with staggeringly precise measurement details. 'Theodor', for example, drew up an extremely detailed plan of a colleague's flat, including measurements not just for the perimeter of the various rooms, but also for the stove and the door opening size (C-2b, pp. 26–9). 'Katrin' reported that a fellow student returned from visits home with many products from the West, ranging 'from cosmetics to pudding mixture' (C-7b, p. 50). Sometimes it is the clumsy way in which this information is recorded which increases its apparent triviality, yet reports of this kind were potentially of considerable use to the Stasi officers, for example, if they were able from a sketch of a flat to decide where to plant bugging devices.

In the majority of cases, the potential harm which could have been caused by such reports was not realised. Former unofficial employees who claim that their reports never caused any harm can, however, never know this for certain. The seemingly harmless pieces of information supplied were like fragments of a mosaic and often only became meaningful when combined with information from other informers. The Stasi did not like to take chances and checked and double-checked information which was considered important. Reports given by informers were, furthermore, not necessarily of immediate use, but were often filed and stored for later application (D-1, p. 5).

Informers were also never supposed to know more than was necessary to obtain the required information and legends were sometimes created by the officers as to why particular information was being requested. These legends ensured that the informers did not gain insight into the 'operative knowledge' of their Stasi officer (D-2, p. 17). Pedagogic material from the JHS underlined this point:

> Even the most experienced unofficial employee should not be able to form a detailed picture of which specific issues are being dealt with in cases, or of which evidence must be obtained and secured, since he only ever has and must only ever have limited insight into the work (D-3, pp. 3–4).

Former unofficial employees often do not consider the potential consequences of this amassing of small, apparently harmless pieces of information when they claim, as do the majority who speak out publicly, that the reports they gave were harmless. Since most of the reports seemed trivial, informers will have been less aware in this pervading atmosphere of banality that they invariably let information slip which was potentially more harmful.

Although often harmless, or at least apparently so, the meetings with the unofficial employees had one chilling objective:

> The goal-oriented processing of those engaged in enemy activities or suspected of such, with the aim of rapidly tracing and ending these activities, as well as quickly and effectively liquidating the individuals concerned (F-5, I, 279).

In rare cases, 'liquidation' literally meant the physical destruction of the enemy, and the songwriter Wolf Biermann found evidence in his files that the Stasi had planned to tamper with his car brakes (I-12). Sometimes the enemy was to be debilitated by mental torture. This could be achieved by a variety of methods. In the case of Gerd Poppe, who was himself under Stasi surveillance, rumours were spread that he was actually working as an informer (I-37). Even after 'state enemies' were forced to leave the GDR, they did not escape the Stasi. When prominent dissident Jürgen Fuchs arrived in West Berlin after being forced to leave the GDR, so too did an informer who had also been in captivity there. It was this man's task to spread false information about any accounts Fuchs might give of the harshly unjust treatment he had received in East Germany prior to his departure (J-27, p. 78). Although only a small proportion of the information supplied by informers was ever used for such measures, when it was it could have grave consequences for those whose existence had become a burden to the Stasi.

Former informers may have an unrealistic idea of how much information they actually gave, since their willingness to compromise their principles and gradually allow more specific and detailed reports to be extracted tended to increase gradually over time. The first reports which informers were asked to give were often fairly general, and it was often only later that they were requested to inform on specific individuals. When 'Theodor' looks back now on his work for the Stasi, he realises how he gradually compromised himself: '... the fact that I was later set directly upon people ... yes ... yes, you know, you just slip into it more and more' (A-2). 'Stephana', too, began her work for the Stasi determined not to make too many compromises. When she signed the written commitment, she informed her Stasi officer that there were specific areas of her life on which she did not wish to give reports. He assured her that the Stasi could accept this. When a superior checked through the file, however, he noted in the margin: 'Why was consent given?' (C-6a, p. 39). The officer in charge of 'Stephana's' case was thus under pressure to encourage her not to withhold any information in which the Stasi might be interested. 'Stephana' does admit that her Stasi officer was skilled at getting her to talk of specific events and casually slipping in questions about particular participants there (A-8). The fact that the Stasi had various sources reporting on these events gave 'Stephana' the impression that he knew everything anyway and that there was no point in trying to keep anything hidden from him: 'Even when I didn't tell him something, I was never actually able to hide anything. They knew, that at such and such a time I had been with the Jehovah's Witnesses, for example' (A-8).

* * *

Despite the apparent triviality of many reports in their files, most informers do seem to have engaged in some more serious sleuthing at some point during their contact with the Stasi. The majority of 'Sonnenblume's' reports, for example, were without doubt overwhelmingly positive character descriptions of her friends and acquaintances. She tells me that she decided only to write positively of others in the hope that perhaps such a report could actually help someone (A-10). Yet, in the course of her contact to the Stasi, 'Sonnenblume' searched through her friends' flat for evidence that they were involved in helping people to escape from the GDR, taking photos which she subsequently handed over to her Stasi officer (C-8a, p. 103). Another example of such sleuthing is found in the case of 'Falke', who is one of many informers who were at some point asked to intensify their friendship with a particular person whom the Stasi wished to place under closer surveillance. In order to achieve this aim 'Falke' used the chance of 'an offer made by [X] to go for a walk in the evening with their wives' (C-3b, II, p. 235). It is also noted that 'Falke' has suggested that he and [X] go fishing together in order that he has the possibility to subsequently give details of the man's holiday cottage (ibid.).

The life of an unofficial employee could, on occasion, even be quite exciting. 'Theodor', for example, was given the task of obtaining a key from a colleague's flat in order that a copy could be made of it. Preparations for this event involved determining the type of lock and at what times the key was left in the door. Apparently, keys were often left in doors with this type of lock, when, for example, as in this case, the children of the family were out playing (A-2). After the plan had been successfully realised, 'Theodor' placed the key on the floor near the flat door to give the impression that children had removed it and thrown it back there. Since the Stasi was keen to check whether this ruse had worked, 'Theodor' was instructed to continue observing the flat in order to determine if the key was left in the door after this incident. If it was, this would suggest that the occupants' suspicions had not been aroused (C-2b, pp. 53–4, 61–2).

A venture such as the one described above often led to scruples being aroused on the part of the informer, and 'Theodor' did, in fact, use the word 'snoop' to refer to himself during our conversation (A-2). He says that, at the time he was active for the Stasi, he did not always consider himself such, but recalled that he certainly did when he was instructed on one occasion to hide in a doorway and monitor whether a man under surveillance received visitors from the West. Of course, it is possible that 'Theodor' may not really have been experiencing scruples at this point, but rather humiliation at being given and carrying out such a lowly task, which he, since he was after all an officer at a military college, may have considered beneath him. Many informers, including 'Theodor', do seem, however, to have suffered from genuine scruples at some point. At the first meeting after her recruitment, 'Sonnenblume' made an attempt to go back on the pledge she had made to the Stasi (C-8b, p. 4). After she was unsuccessful in this venture, she began reluctantly to co-operate with the wishes of the officer in whose charge she had been placed, but the doubts remained, and at a later date he noted that 'Sonnenblume' had told him how she had experienced scruples when gathering information for a specific report (ibid. p. 84). The documents in the files suggest that, at least occasionally, most of those with whom I spoke did express doubts to their Stasi officer. 'Rolf', for example, experienced scruples very early on in his contact to the Stasi after writing a report about someone for the first time. The officer asked 'Rolf' if he felt like a snoop: 'He hesitantly said yes, at which point the difference between a snoop and an unofficial Stasi employee was explained to the candidate' (C-1a, p. 278). The recruiting officers succeeded at this stage in reassuring 'Rolf', but during the following months this informer's doubts continued to resurface. The whole nature of 'Rolf's' meetings with the Stasi was suspect to him:

> And I have to say, that whereas it all had a sort of official character while it was taking place in the town hall, with, yes, we were in a place of work, then we started meeting at a flat in [X], that was one of those secret flats, where in the afternoon the table is suddenly set, and we were to be there at 4 o'clock for example, and there's cake on the table, and coffee, and then somehow, you know, you feel something's not right here. That was always the impression I had, you go up the back stairs and are not to be seen beforehand, and you have to be very careful that no one you know sees you. When I went there I was told to say that I was going to a meeting, and it all had a sort of criminal element to it (A-1).

'Rolf' soon broke off contact with the Stasi on his own initiative. For other potential informers, the doubts were too strong at the time of planned recruitment to get involved at all. One man simply told the recruiting officer that he didn't want to become a 'Stasi snoop' and perhaps have 'to grass on his mates' (J-80, p. 167). The officer concluded: 'Further contact meetings are necessary with the candidate to convince him politically and ideologically that the concept of a "snoop" is a term of the enemy, created to be used against the working class and their achievements' (J-80, p. 167). These further talks were, however, to no avail, and the man was never registered as an informer.

In summary, although there was a considerable amount of discrepancy between theory and practice, the Stasi's work with unofficial employees followed, in general, the basic principles of the guidelines set down. Informers were instrumental in supplying the Stasi with information which could potentially be used to destroy or neutralise the enemy. Often this information had an apparently banal character to it, and most informers thus claim that their actions never harmed anyone. It may well be true that no direct harm was ever caused by individual informers, but they can never be sure that this was the case. Giving seemingly banal information could have serious consequences, either at the time of reporting or at a later date. This was especially true when information was amassed from a variety of sources. Furthermore, there were moments in many informers' careers when they cannot have been anything but acutely aware of the potential harm which could be caused to others as a result of the reports given. For this reason many unofficial employees experienced, at least periodically, doubts or scruples about their actions.

* * *

One of the most significant factors in determining whether candidates would agree initially to co-operate with the Stasi, and whether they would continue the work in spite of some doubts, was the relationship between informers and their Stasi officers. The Stasi placed great importance on the well-being of its unofficial employees, and officers were advised to keep sight of the fact that 'the unofficial employees are most directly confronted with the enemy and carry the main burden of this work' (D-4, I, p. 55). The informer was thus to be treated at all times with the utmost respect, and officers were instructed to develop 'genuine human bonds' with their informers (D-9, p. 47). The establishment of such a genuine interpersonal relationship was thought to be of considerable importance in the overall effectiveness of the work. When questioned on the factors which they considered to have most positively influenced their co-operation with the Stasi, 84.1 per cent of informers felt that a good relationship to their Stasi officer was significant (D-6, II, Appendix 32). In comparison, only 6.1 per cent ticked the factor of 'material recognition' as being positively significant (ibid.). It should not be ruled out, however, that the low percentage of informers who identified material reward as positively influencing their work may be partly accounted for by the fact that some informers were wary of admitting that they valued such rewards, imagining perhaps that this response would be regarded unfavourably.

The 'genuine human bond' which the Stasi officer strove to cultivate with the unofficial employees in his care could be manifested in various forms and intensities. Some informers claim that they regarded their officer as a colleague and, therefore, an equal. 'Theodor', for example, had great respect for his first officer, but did not even consider this man's successor an equal, describing him as a loser with low intellectual ability (A-2). The relationship of informers to their Stasi officer was, however, only ever superficially one of equals. When put to the test, the power hierarchy was soon evident. It was the officer who dictated what form the meetings were to take and which tasks were to be carried out. Despite his lack of respect for the man's intellectual capabilities, 'Theodor' and the majority of unofficial employees generally complied with these demands. 'Thaer', for example, may well have considered his officer an equal in many respects, as he claims, but since 'Thaer' was a West German citizen who was betraying his country by conspiring with the Stasi, the power that this man held over him was considerable. 'Thaer' describes the fear he experienced at the thought of the West German authorities finding out about his secret life, and his officer was quick to remind him just how serious the matter was. When, in somewhat mysterious circumstances, 'Thaer' lost a briefcase fitted with a hidden compartment which had been given to him by the

Stasi, he remembers the chill he experienced when he was told in response to this news: '"You should be shot for that"' (A-5). Moments such as these were, however, relatively rare, and the prevailing ambience of this particular informer/Stasi officer bond, as of many others, may well have been that of a relationship of equals.

In some cases, the relationship between the informer and the officer went beyond that of colleagues and was perceived, at least on the part of the informer, as a friendship. 'Stephana' said that she felt she could talk to her officer 'like a good friend' (A-8). Evidence suggests that 'Stephana's' sentiments were shared by a significant number of informers. In one study, ten out of twenty-one unofficial employees compared their Stasi officer to a friend or even best friend (D-8, p. 7). In reality, any trust or openness which was established through this friendship remained ultimately one-sided. The officers were instructed to give informers the impression that the relationship was a friendship, but since informers were, for example, never to know more than was necessary to carry out the desired task, they were constantly being manipulated. When one newly-recruited unofficial employee decided to withdraw the written commitment he had made, he insisted upon destroying the document personally. It was noted that the man seemed composed and satisfied as he burned the paper in the oven in the presence of his officer (F-11, pp. 210–11). The man did not seem to guess that the declaration of commitment had long since been copied and filed. The imbalance in such a relationship is further highlighted by the fact that, at the beginning of every informer's file, a list was drawn up of the names of the Stasi officers who were known to the informers and of the names by which he or she knew these people. Sometimes these were the real names of the officers concerned, sometimes they were merely cover names. In contrast, the Stasi officers generally had access to detailed information on almost every aspect of informers' public and private lives.

In cases where informers considered their Stasi officers to be some kind of friend or equal it was not, of course, the reality of the situation which was instrumental in achieving the best results for the Stasi, but rather the way in which the bond was perceived. Every effort was made to make the informer feel comfortable during meetings, and this cosy atmosphere, and the impression of friendship that it helped to simulate, perhaps lulled them into a false sense of familiar congeniality. This relatively relaxed state may have resulted in informers being no longer as wary as might otherwise have been the case and they may have let information slip which they had not planned to. 'Stephana' says that, particularly since her Stasi officer regularly expressed opinions which were critical of the state and which she considered genuine, she felt that her conversations with him were clearly divided into an official section and a section where she was talking to him privately and as a friend (A-8). With hindsight, 'Stephana' now realises that information which she gave in what she considered to be the unofficial part of their meetings was probably used in the reports compiled afterwards. 'Katrin' similarly recognises the potential danger in feeling too relaxed with a Stasi officer. She remembers having a better rapport with the first of two men who were responsible for her. She describes her meetings with this first man as 'relatively relaxed – perhaps this made it more dangerous, I can't really say now' (A-9). The danger for these informers lay in the fact that when the atmosphere seemed to be relaxed and friendly they tended to forget that the ultimate purpose of the meetings was for the Stasi officer to extract information from them, rather than to have a pleasant conversational exchange.

'Sonnenblume's' feelings for her Stasi officer went beyond those of platonic friendship, and she describes him as 'a devilish magnet' for whom she experienced an intense physical and mental attraction (J-110, p. 260). Since she considered him to be both good-looking and intelligent, she felt flattered by his attentions. After a meeting in January 1978, her officer certainly did note in his report that 'Sonnenblume' had told him that she had been very much looking forward to his visit since she had not been able to get out much due to the bad weather conditions (C-8b, p. 16). 'Sonnenblume' admits, however, that she perhaps exaggerates today just how strong her attraction to this man was in order to justify having worked for the Stasi (A-10). It is, nevertheless, the case that when she was assigned a new officer, whom she did not find so attractive, 'Sonnenblume' did break off the contact with the Stasi. The role of the Stasi officer as an admirer is clearly one which was, in general, potentially more intense for female informers. 'Stephana' also felt flattered by the attentions of her officer and regarded the gifts which she received as personal and as coming directly from him rather than from the institution for which he worked (A-8).

A rather more intensified form of the informer/officer relationship was apparent in the case of Monika Haeger. Haeger had been a full-time unofficial employee, reporting on the activities of the opposition groups with which she was involved, such as Women for Peace. Two of the women whom she reported on, Katja Havemann and Irena Kukutz, later interviewed Haeger at length about her work for the Stasi and subsequently published extracts of these conversations (J-45). Haeger was an orphan who had spent a lonely and problematic childhood. As an adult, she had psychological difficulties and had been seeing a therapist before she began working for the Stasi. When active as an informer, however, Haeger claimed that she no longer needed this therapy, as she felt that she had found a sort of substitute therapist in her Stasi officer, 'Detlef', whom she could call at any time of the day or night (ibid. p. 43).

Monika Haeger's psychological dependence was intense. The majority of informers did not consider their Stasi officer to be playing the role of an analyst. The officer was, nevertheless, someone with whom many informers had the opportunity to discuss personal affairs. The guidelines for the work with unofficial employees do after all stipulate that a conversation about personal matters is to be an integral part of all meetings (J-62, p. 223). The officers were to be aware that any personal problems which the informer had could hinder their ability to fulfil the required duties: 'For this reason the officer must be aware of the unofficial employee's problems and build up a relationship to him that sees him turning in trust to the officer in personal matters too' (ibid. p. 228). The Stasi officers were then expected to get to know their unofficial employees intimately. In a study for the JHS, Stasi researcher Wardezki designed a detailed table of information about the physical appearance of unofficial employees, which he suggested could be completed by all officers in charge of unofficial employees (D-7, II, pp. 59–104). Each part of the informer's face was to be described in detail, and the section under nose alone asked for information on the top, bone, tip, width and height, as well as on any other defining features. There were eleven possibilities to choose from to describe the gait of the person concerned, and numerous habits were listed which he or she might engage in, such as the picking of nose and/or ears, and the rubbing of ears and/or hands. The fact that Wardezki could even dream up this rather unrealistic chart indicates that it was considered self-explanatory that Stasi officers be intensely familiar with their individual informers.

The information which the unofficial employees gave during the conversation about personal matters was often noted down in the report of the meeting, allowing the officers to keep track of the personal circumstances of those in their charge. The officers were sometimes able to do more than just listen to any problems their informers had and could, if deemed necessary, actually intervene in their private life. When 'Rolf' mentioned the fact that his mother had been waiting to move out of her dilapidated flat for quite some time, the matter was quickly resolved with the necessary authorities (A-1). Apparently without her direct request, 'Stephana's' officer arranged that her divorce proceedings be speeded up (C-6a, p. 95). Perhaps the role of the Stasi officer towards the unofficial employee can, at moments such as these, be best described as that of a mentor.

Intervention by officers in the private life of informers not only meant that they would consequently be in a better position to carry out the assigned tasks competently, but also created a debt which increased their bond to the Stasi. This bond was, by its nature, often intense since, in some cases, the Stasi officer was the only person who knew of informers' contacts to the Stasi, and they could only hope that they would never be betrayed. This was an issue which caused some informers considerable worry. 'Stephana' was concerned that her boyfriend would be furious if he found out that she was working for the Stasi and asked if she would be given support if her Stasi connections were to become known in her circle of acquaintances. She told her Stasi officer that she was worried that the Stasi would leave her in the lurch if such a situation were to arise (C-6a, p. 104). When 'Rolf' expressed doubts about the consequences of being discovered to be working for the Stasi, he was assured, ironically given today's situation, that no-one outside the organisation would ever find out about this contact (C-1a, p. 279).

Some informers did break the code of silence they had taken and told, for example, their partner of their Stasi contacts. Yet, even in these cases, the Stasi officer remained the only individual who really knew what went on at these secret meetings. Andreas Sinakowski describes the loneliness of being a Stasi informer, and the feeling that 'the only escape from this isolation is to talk to your Stasi officer' (J-88, p. 77). Hendrik Melle likewise makes the point that the only person he could talk to about being an informer was 'my Stasi', as he rather fondly refers to his officer: 'Because the only one whom I could talk to about it was my Stasi. Trusting anyone else with this information would have only created another dependency situation. No one else came as close to me as my Stasi officer' (J-56, p. 156). A further example of this intense dependency comes from Herbert K., a former full-time unofficial employee:

> I worked for the Stasi for thirty years, fifteen of them as an investigator. That was sometimes pretty boring. You didn't have any contact to anyone, you couldn't have any form of exchange with your colleagues, only with your Stasi officer. You worked from home, from where you had to write your reports, you couldn't go to any work events, since your identity was to remain secret from other employees (J-39, p. 58).

The Stasi officer was, then, for many informers, their only true accomplice. Their relief at meetings of suddenly no longer having to lead a double life must have been significant. This aspect of the informer/Stasi officer relationship could only work in the Stasi's favour, when, as a consequence of the welcomed sense of complicity, informers were less wary about what they said to their officer than they perhaps intended to be.

In summary, the bond between the Stasi officer and the informer was fundamental to the effectiveness of their work together. This bond could take on varying degrees of intensity, but the informer was always necessarily dependent on the Stasi officer to some extent. Lienhard Wawrzyn notes that he spoke to many former unofficial employees who wished to meet their Stasi officer again (J-101, p. 26). Several of those whom I spoke to also expressed this interest. 'Rolf' said that he would like to ask his officer if he had been aware that 'Rolf' and the man on whom he was reporting were actually conspiring against the Stasi (A-1). 'Thaer' claimed that he would like to have met up with his Stasi officer, whom he had considered in some ways to be a friend, in order simply to talk to him (A-5). 'Stephana' likewise feels a certain personal loss at being no longer able to meet with her officer, whom, after all, she compared to a good 'buddy' (A-8). It would be interesting to know whether these Stasi officers would be equally keen to meet their former unofficial employees, whether they too feel a sense of loss that they can no longer do so, and to discover how they previously regarded the relationship to their informers. The silence, however, which is found on the part of the majority of these former Stasi officers severely limits such avenues of investigation.

5

'IF ONLY I HAD KNOWN'

Breaking the bond

In the vast majority of cases where an informer's file was shelved, the decision to end the contact was taken by the Stasi and not the informer. Such a move was usually made when the informer was considered no longer suitable for the task at hand or that the task itself had become superfluous. In 71 per cent of 2,431 cases where an informer's file was shelved in the area of Rostock between January 1987 and October 1989, the main reasons given were: the contact had no potential; the informer was not suited to the job; he or she was too old or ill; he or she had been promoted to a full-time unofficial employee (J-63, pp. 123–4). A further 8 per cent of cases came to an end because the informer was judged to be dishonest, and 3 per cent were released from their duties when they were found to have broken their oath of silence about working for the Stasi (ibid. p. 123). In only 16 per cent of cases did unofficial employees end the contact on their own initiative (ibid.). Similar figures are given for the area of Frankfurt/Oder for the period spanning 1981 to 1985 (ibid. p. 124). Several key factors contributed to the fact that so few informers made the break from the Stasi, despite the fact that many suffered, at least periodically, from scruples about their actions and were often no longer convinced that they served any justifiable purpose.

* * *

In 1953, Ernst Wollweber, Erich Mielke's predecessor, explicitly instructed his officers that good work on the part of the unofficial employees was to be rewarded (F-5, I, 61). Although most did not receive a regular wage for their services, many were rewarded in the form of financial bonuses or gifts. These were generally awarded on occasions such as the anniversary of the founding of the GDR, on informers' birthdays, or after they had been seen to successfully carry out a challenging assignment. The gifts were, somewhat ironically, occasionally in the form of goods which were not easily attainable in the GDR, such as flowers or specific books, and as such were often only too willingly accepted. Indeed, when I visited them, several of those with whom I spoke showed me items which they had been given by their Stasi officers. Informers often felt flattered to receive such gifts, especially when they were carefully chosen to reflect their personal taste and interests. Both 'Stephana' and 'Sonnenblume' told of how they liked to think of these gifts as coming from their Stasi officers rather than from the organisation for which they worked (A-8, A-10). If informers were able to convince themselves that this was the case, they not only experienced a sense of flattery, but were also able to partly diminish any feelings of guilt which might otherwise result from accepting material rewards.

Material rewards were thus influential in intensifying the bond of an unofficial employee to the Stasi, not so much because of their objective value, but rather as a result of the fact that, by accepting them, informers further entangled and compromised themselves. It is perhaps for this reason that 'Fuchs' claims to have been reluctant to accept the financial bonuses which he received during his eleven years of service for the Stasi. 'Fuchs' claims that he told his Stasi officer that he did not wish to be financially rewarded: 'At first I always used to say, "What's that for? It goes without saying. You don't need to give me any money. It only amounts to about 3 or 5 per cent of my work" ' (A-6). 'Fuchs' claims that his Stasi officer insisted, however, that he take the money, telling him that he should buy something for his children if he did not wish to spend it on himself. At such times as 'Fuchs' was not receiving money for his actions, it was perhaps easier for him to use the internal justification that his work with the Stasi was simply part of his normal working life. Today he possibly exaggerates his reluctance to accept the money in order to justify his work for the Stasi as having been motivated by a sense of duty and not by self-interest: 'Because that's the point I was always trying to make – that it was a completely normal working relationship for us, and that it was really just part of the job' (A-6). When an informer such as 'Fuchs' did receive money or other material goods, it may thus have served only to increase any uneasiness experienced, and to undermine the sense of a meaningful purpose which had been cultivated at the time of recruitment.

As previously discussed, the Stasi's guidelines discouraged officers from establishing a relationship with their informers which was motivated by the receipt of material reward, and encouraged them to work on educating the informers in order to convince them of the political and moral necessity of the task. The officers did not, however, always heed these guidelines. When 'Reiner's' officer applied for a 5,000 mark bonus for his informer, his application was initially rejected on the grounds that such a reward was not in line with the principles of the 1979 guidelines (C-4a, I, p. 332). Yet the claim does appear to have been finally accepted as, soon after this application, 'Reiner' signed a receipt for this amount (C-4a, I, p. 333). This was a princely sum which 'Reiner' was perhaps more than happy to receive, but Stasi researchers Seidler and Schmidt suggest that officers were not always successful in giving their unofficial employees the type of reward they most wished. When informers were asked to specify which form of recognition they considered most effective in their work with the Stasi, 38.1 per cent ticked the category 'praise', 23.1 per cent considered some form of 'state decoration' most valuable, and only 21.5 per cent named a 'financial reward' as most significant (D-6, I, p. 134). When the officers were asked in the same study about the type of recognition they actually gave the informers in their charge, this question produced quite different results: 21.9 per cent reported using primarily praise, only 1.5 per cent reported using official recognition, whereas a financial reward was, at 58 per cent, by far the most favoured form of recognition (ibid.). It is likely that some informers felt that to state that they considered financial recognition as the most effective reward for their work would constitute an undesired response. Perhaps these people were consequently not entirely honest about the extent to which they valued such recognition. Yet, conversely, the Stasi officers who had been instructed not to use material rewards as the primary form of recognition had nothing to gain by claiming to do so more often than was actually the case. Interestingly, and perhaps significantly, the authors of this particular study see its validity confirmed by the fact that 15.4 per cent of the informers questioned admitted having told their spouses about the contact to the Stasi, although they had pledged not to do so (D-6, I, p. 12).

In summary, most informers did not receive sufficient material recognition for this to be a significant motive for continuing to work for the Stasi. The material recognition which many did receive on a fairly regular basis throughout the course of their work did, nevertheless, have a strong bonding effect. By accepting such gifts or rewards, informers compromised themselves further and thus intensified their entanglement with the Stasi. Although they enjoyed the flattery or the advantages of such recognition, this was not necessarily a feeling with which they felt entirely comfortable. 'Sonnenblume', for example, describes how disgusted she was at herself after she accepted some West German marks from her Stasi officer, which she herself had requested in order to buy spare parts for her wheelchair.

'Sonnenblume' considered such action as symptomatic of her 'moral downfall' (J-110, p. 261).

Possibly more significant than the material advantages deriving from working for the Stasi were the potential social benefits of having found favour with those in power. The negative aspect of such a liaison for the informer was the fear of the possible repercussions of deciding not to continue the work. 'Katrin' told of how she had decided at one point while she was still studying in Leningrad to break off the contact with the Stasi. The officer in charge of her case was able to persuade her not to do so. When I asked her how he succeeded in doing this, she replied:

> You know, when you ask me now, I don't know anymore. I know that I had a sort of feeling that it wouldn't be good to leave on bad terms, a sort of intuition. [. . .] Perhaps it was even because I was concerned about what it would do to my career, that's stupid. [. . .] Somehow I got it into my head that I could just quietly get out, without being put under pressure. I didn't want there to be a sudden break (A-9).

Although 'Katrin's' fears that her career could be thwarted if she were to make a break from the Stasi may have seemed well-founded, in the vast majority of cases any informers who did take this step did not suffer any serious negative repercussions for doing so. Yet, in some sense this fact is irrelevant. The more important question is not whether those who took this step actually suffered, but rather whether they believed that they would. Christopher Browning concludes that the men of the Reserve Police Battalion 101, which was responsible for large-scale round-ups and executions of Jews during World War Two, cannot be said to have been under 'putative duress', since those who did not feel capable of participating in the mass shootings were granted permission to excuse themselves (J-18, pp. 170–1). Daniel Goldhagen's controversial work confirms this finding. Goldhagen discusses the case of Lieutenant Buchmann, who was the only man to make use of Major Trapp's offer to all the officers that it was not mandatory for them or their men to take part in the shootings. Buchmann found little sympathy for his stance among the other officers, but his decision to make use of this freedom was tolerated, and Goldhagen provocatively concludes: 'Lieutenant Buchmann did not kill because pressure was not applied; the others killed anyway, because pressure was unnecessary' (J-30, p. 250). Although it would be grossly inappropriate to equate the deeds of the men of the notorious Police Battalion 101 directly with those of the average Stasi informer, a comparison is possible. Both the informers and the men in the Battalion were engaged in actions which undoubtedly violated certain basic moral codes, but which were officially, if not always explicitly, sanctioned by the state. Moreover, for a substantial number of informers, a situation of putative duress, albeit in a mild form, did exist. This was particularly the case for those who had been recruited under duress in the first instance, such as 'Stephana' and 'Sonnenblume'. These individuals had, after all, been threatened with legal action if they did not agree to co-operate. Many unofficial employees had also signed a written commitment in which they acknowledged that there would be legal repercussions for breaking the agreement. Most informers, however, actually put themselves under putative duress, by imagining that the consequences of disentangling themselves from the clutches of the Stasi would be potentially grave, even when direct threats had not actually been made. By convincing themselves that they had to work for the Stasi, the informer reduced personal responsibility for doing so. The state of putative duress was then one which allowed many to alleviate, at least partially, irksome doubts.

The work of the psychologist Stanley Milgram is interesting in this context. In his work on obedience to authority, Milgram found deference to be a 'deeply ingrained behaviour tendency' (cited in J-18, p. 171). Milgram's subjects were led to believe that they were involved in a learning experiment, in which they were to inflict increasingly powerful electric shocks on the 'learners' whenever their responses were incorrect. The 'learners' were in reality not being subjected to shocks at all, but were actors who were simulating the crying noises which were relayed to the unsuspecting subject. When encouraged to do so by the experimenter, two-thirds of these subjects continued to inflict shocks which they believed were causing extreme pain. Milgram concluded that, once they have begun the experiment, subjects become more and more entangled and disobedience becomes increasingly difficult and unlikely: 'The "situational obligation" or etiquette makes refusal appear improper, rude, or even an immoral breach of obligation' (J-18, p. 173). Milgram went on to apply his findings in an interpretation of the behaviour of many ordinary citizens in Nazi Germany, concluding that 'men are led to kill with little difficulty' (ibid.). His results can also facilitate an understanding of why, in a considerably less extreme situation, so many unofficial employees continued to work with the Stasi. Several variations of the experiment are interesting in this context. The more physically distant the subject was from the 'learner', the higher the rate of compliance. Furthermore, if the subject had to actually force the person's hand onto the shock-plate, compliance to extreme levels dropped to 30 per cent. Since the Stasi pieced small fragments of information together from different sources as in a mosaic, informers were very rarely witness to any directly harmful consequences of their actions. Had they been able to see how their apparently trivial information could cause harm to others, one could suppose that compliance would have dropped significantly. A further variation of the experiment found that if the instruction to give the shocks was delivered by a figure who did not appear to hold a position of authority, compliance rates dropped to zero. Stasi officers were powerful representatives of the state, and the informers' awareness of this might well have been a significant factor in influencing their behaviour, regardless of their own political convictions.

Informers were often influenced in their decision to carry on working for the Stasi by their own sometimes unquestioning deference to authority. 'Theodor', who describes himself as having 'a more than average respect for authority', said that since his colleagues at the military college had pledged to have no contact to the West, his work in helping to detect whether they were breaking this oath was in some ways justified: 'The people had, yes, they had signed a written agreement, that ... that they wouldn't do it. In that respect I felt that I was in the right' (A-2). Not all informers were quite as respectful of authority as 'Theodor', but many, as a consequence of a series of 'binding factors' and 'cementing mechanisms', found it increasingly difficult to disentangle themselves from a situation, which, once in motion, took on its own momentum (Milgram, J-18, p. 173).

* * *

The sense that there was a meaningful purpose to their actions was generally stronger for informers at the point of recruitment than as a motivating factor for continued co-operation, but the Stasi was keen to preserve the belief in the moral and political necessity of the work. The political education of the unofficial employees was, therefore, to be an important component of meetings. 'Reiner', for example, was given the task of studying the history of the SED in preparation for one meeting (C-4a, I, 284). 'Reiner' was a full-time unofficial employee, and perhaps the officer was particularly concerned to ensure that political education was a continuous feature of the work with this informer. In other cases, the evidence from the files indicates that most of the political work was carried out in the period immediately before and after recruitment. In later documents, there is little mention of political discussions with informers, and both 'Rolf' and 'Falke' recounted experiencing the section of the meetings which was occasionally devoted to a discussion of political issues as sterile and patronising (A-1, A-3).

Informers themselves were, however, often keen to keep believing that the contacts had a justifiable purpose. Those who were unable to summon the resolve to break off the contact with the Stasi strove to convince themselves of the legitimacy of their actions, even if this required an increasing amount of self-deception. The Stasi was, of course, generally just as concerned that the informers remain active, and in this sense both parties had a common goal and worked hard at deceiving themselves and each other in its pursuit.

* * *

The psychologist Hans-Joachim Maaz argues that most GDR citizens were only able to conform publicly in situations which were totally at odds with their private convictions as a result of a split in personality (J-54, p. 76). Maaz is not alone in explaining conformity in the GDR in terms of a form of schizophrenia. Speaking to the Enquete Commission, Walter Schilling said that informers 'all had to lead two lives. In the long term this fostered a shocking and incomprehensible schizophrenia' (F-13, p. 97).

For some informers, the discrepancy between actual behaviour and private perception of self could certainly at times be particularly extreme. This is highlighted by the paradox inherent in the fact that many were active in the opposition scene at the same time as they worked with an organisation who aimed to undermine such activities. Rainer Eppelmann found this phenomenon baffling as he came to terms with the fact that Wolfgang Schnur seemed to be able to develop genuine friendships with those on whom he was simultaneously reporting: 'It sounds ridiculous, but even today I still think that Wolfgang Schnur used to consider himself our friend' (J-23, p. 294). There is no doubt, as this example demonstrates, that many informers were able to carry on a form of double life, reporting on those whose friendship they still valued. Yet it was perhaps not so much that informers had two personalities, one of an average GDR citizen and one of an evil Stasi informer, but rather that their behaviour represented a more intense form of a common tendency to opportunistic conformity (see Chapter 8). Furthermore, state ideology in the GDR emphasised the collective rather than the individual. Self-reflection and analysis were not cultivated and propagated to the same extent as is the case in the West. One possible consequence of this tendency was that individuals did not engage in such intense introspection, deeply analysing past and present perceptions of self and others. At the same time as this tendency was encouraged by the fact that the system focused on the collective, it was simultaneously reinforced and confirmed by the individual, since it offered a feasible way of coping with life under a dictatorship. It was, then, rather more the case that a behaviour pattern of opportunistic conformity, combined with a lack of self-reflection and analysis, allowed informers to engage in apparently contradictory behaviours, rather than that several selves were at play within the one individual. For Andreas Sinakowski, for example, the process of 'forgetting' that he was attending certain events as part of his duties as a Stasi informer was conscious and deliberate, and usually did not require too much effort. Describing a social gathering at the house of someone he was supposed to observe, Sinakowski writes: 'It didn't seem real that I was there on a mission from the Stasi. Two drinks later I'd forgotten all about it' (J-88, p. 75).

Perhaps Sinakowski had become so used to this party routine that it no longer seemed strange to him. As stated previously, Christopher Browning concluded that the *Ordinary Men* of Reserve Police Battalion 101 were able to carry out the killings because for these men, 'normality itself had become exceedingly abnormal' (J-18, xix). This factor does, indeed, help explain why it was that most informers continued to work for the Stasi even after they were neither under direct pressure to do so, nor sufficiently convinced of the moral or political purpose of doing so. Since the meetings with the Stasi officers generally took place at regular intervals, it was relatively easy for informers to integrate the contact into their daily routine. In addition, most officers did not adhere to the Stasi's guidelines, which explicitly discouraged them from establishing a set pattern in the contact with their unofficial employees. This fact meant that many informers could continue their work for the Stasi without ever giving it much thought or attention. Generally the tasks assigned to any one informer tended to be similar in nature. Once they had come to terms with their actions, the contact could continue almost indefinitely, since it had become part of a set and predictable routine. Doubts did arise on the part of the individual informer from time to time but could generally be put to rest relatively easily by the officer concerned.

* * *

Those belonging to the minority of informers who did sooner or later break off the contact to the Stasi on their own initiative were generally surprised at how easy this move was. 'Sonnenblume' claims that if she had realised how easy it was to break the bond, she would have done so much sooner: 'If only I had known how easy it was. [. . .] But you were so afraid, you took the threats too seriously' (A-10). As a rule, the Stasi was not interested in continuing contacts with those who proved themselves unwilling or unreliable. If only more informers had seen a standard closing report for an unofficial employee's file, perhaps they would have been more likely to break off the contact. These closing reports named the following possible reasons for a case being shelved:

Breaking of oath of silence
Refusal to cooperate
Arrest in the West
Dishonesty/Unreliability
Illness/old age/death
Unsuitability/lack of potential
Illegal departure from the GDR
Change of work/address
Re-employment as a full-time MfS employee
Re-classification to a GMS
Being guilty of enemy/criminal activity, leading to surveillance or legal proceedings
Personal reasons, official connections, other reasons (C-1a, p. 314).

The above list shows that the Stasi certainly reckoned with informers taking the initiative to end the contact for a number of reasons. In reality, as discussed, it was the officer in charge of the case who most often made the decision to bring the contact to an end. Very few informers ever realised that they needed only 'categorically refuse' to continue the contact to the Stasi in order to break free (J-62, pp. 280–1). Most considered themselves bound until they were released of their duties, fearing at the same time the imagined repercussions of falling into disfavour and, consequently, having their work discontinued. The Stasi was able to keep its informers without much effort, since informers effectively made themselves captive, leading one former Stasi officer to comment: 'They only need to give a big push and they'd be rid of us. But they don't have the guts. We control them and they let themselves be controlled. It takes two to tango' (J-33, p. 77).

6

POLITICIANS AS INFORMERS

MANFRED STOLPE: A MAN OF THE CHURCH?

> What country ever gets off to such a good a start with a treaty like this?
>
> (Lothar de Maizière, J-38, p. 196)

The irony of these words, spoken on the occasion of the unification of the two Germanys on 3 October 1990, by the man who had been the last head of state of the GDR, could no longer be concealed a mere two months later. Fresh evidence from the Stasi files meant that Lothar de Maizière was no longer able to deny that he had worked as an unofficial employee under the name of 'Czerny', and he was forced to step out of the political arena. The absurdity of the fact that the unification treaty had been countersigned by a man who had worked with the East German State Security Service was to be a feature of the political and cultural climate of the following years. No political party remained untouched. Dirk Schneider from the Green Party was found to have worked as an informer, so too Ibrahim Böhme, who helped to found the East German Social Democrats, and Kerstin Kaiser from the PDS. Most of the politicians who were discovered to have worked for the Stasi were forced to resign, but some were able to remain in office, notably Rolf Kutzmutz of the PDS, who succeeded in being voted in as mayor of Potsdam using the provocative election slogan, 'My biography didn't just begin in 1989', a tactic which, it was suggested, had lost him 10 per cent of the vote, but gained him 20 per cent (I-48).

The case which resulted in the most extensive discussion of a politician's Stasi connections was that of Dr. Manfred Stolpe. The debate was sparked off by none other than Stolpe himself with the publication of his book *Schwieriger Aufbruch* (J-91). Stolpe claimed that his intention in writing this book was to document 'the perspectives I have gained over the years on the power structures in place in the GDR' (ibid. pp. 111–12). In the book, Stolpe admitted to having gained this insight by virtue of the fact that since the 1970s he had attempted to achieve his political aims 'by going the roundabout way via the Stasi' (ibid. p. 121). Following this admission, which coincided with the Stasi Document Law coming into force, the Stolpe Committee was set up and began its work on 27 February 1992. The official task of the Committee was stated as follows: 'To clarify the nature of the contacts held by the Premier [of Brandenburg], Dr. Manfred Stolpe, to state organs in the GDR, to the SED and to the State Security Service, and to investigate the accusations made in this context' (F-2, I, p. 2). Over the next two years, the Committee heard the testimonies of numerous prominent politicians and theologians from both the former GDR and FRG, as well as those of former Stasi officers. The Stolpe debate was given extensive media coverage, and it was proposed that its outcome would go a long way to deciding 'on the course set after the collapse of the GDR' (J-70, p. 51).

A great number of East Germans identified with Manfred Stolpe and did not want to see him forced to resign. Stolpe's party, the Social Democrats (SPD), also had a clear interest in ensuring that the popular Stolpe remain in power, whilst at the same time trying to preserve its political credibility by not being seen to confront the problematic legacy of the GDR in too lenient a fashion. This posed a problem for the likes of Wolfgang Thierse, who had to be seen to support his party's stance on the Stolpe debate, but whose contemporaries among the ranks of the citizens' rights groups of the former GDR criticised him severely for not speaking out against Stolpe. A heated debate flared up, for example, between Thierse and Jürgen Fuchs when the former refused to speak out against Stolpe, arguing that to do so would be to go against the principle of innocent until proven guilty (I-67; I-68).

By contrast, Günter Nooke from the Bündnis '90 party was certainly not prepared to let the immediate political agenda stand in the way of his belief that Stolpe should not remain in office. Nooke threatened to leave the Stolpe Committee in summer 1992 in protest at the fact that an interim report had been passed without discussion. He returned after the summer break when the report was withdrawn but remained dissatisfied. In March 1993, Nooke directly accused Stolpe of having lied in the hearings. The SPD demanded that he withdraw this accusation, and his refusal to do so led to the end of the coalition government in Brandenburg (F-2, I; C. 2). Nooke was largely unsuccessful in his attempt to find support for his breakaway party, Bündnis, and in the end it seemed, at this point, as though Nooke and not Stolpe had been forced to sacrifice his political career as a result of the latter's Stasi connections.

The Stolpe debate was thus one with obvious ramifications in the volatile political climate of post-unification Germany. The fact that Stolpe was not forced to resign, and remains to this day in office, is clearly a significant victory for the SPD, who fared so badly in the first elections after the fall of the Wall. The PDS have also benefited from the outcome of the Stolpe debate. If Stolpe can remain in power after admitting to having had dealings with the Stasi, then it is possible that other such cases, of which there are many within the ranks of the PDS, will be viewed more leniently than would have been the case if he had been forced into resignation.

Manfred Stolpe was undoubtedly one of the most influential representatives of the church in the GDR, so much so that Friedrich Schorlemmer claimed: 'I cannot imagine what we, the church in the GDR, would have been without Manfred Stolpe' (J-82, p. 276). Stolpe succeeded in establishing and nurturing links to leading politicians and theologians in both the East and West, and many were content to benefit from these connections without questioning to what extent he might be collaborating with those in power in order to preserve and facilitate them. A declaration by leading church members on this issue read as follows:

> We entrusted the handling of all sensitive and difficult questions to Manfred Stolpe regarding the relationship between the state and the church, without specifying which individual steps should be taken (F-2, I, p. 62).

Many within the ranks of the church had thus been content to turn a blind eye to the methods which Stolpe was using to achieve his goals. Even Rainer Eppelmann, who strongly advocated Stolpe's resignation, had, for example, previously accepted a typewriter which Stolpe had acquired 'from the West through some secret channels or other' (J-23, p. 125). When it had been made explicit that such an undertaking did, of course, involve considerable dealings with representatives of the Stasi, Eppelmann began to seriously question Stolpe's credibility as a politician and as a representative of the church.

In the GDR, the church had often attracted those who were reluctant to conform to state policies and, particularly in the late 1980s, had served as a meeting place for diverse groups and individuals who were becoming increasingly disillusioned with the status quo. In this sense the church had fostered the opposition movement in the GDR, not so much because its representatives had been at the forefront of anti-state activities, but rather because it had provided a forum for individuals to gather and to establish connections which they then used to develop their own opposition activities. Theology was, furthermore, one of the few subjects open to those who, often for political reasons, had been refused entry to other courses of study in the GDR. Under the roof of the church many individuals were thus to be found who were dissatisfied with the system. The church itself, however, acted more as a regulating force, as an integral and established part of the system, and in this sense did nothing to challenge the existing order. Former members of the Women for Peace group, Ulrike Poppe and Katrin Eigenfeld, stressed that the church was not interested in promoting opposition activities in the GDR, but had rather suppressed true opposition. By always encouraging those involved in opposition groups to act within the law, the church, they argued, had in fact functioned as a censor (F-14, pp. 119–22).

The fact that the church as an institution was well integrated into the existing power structures became even more evident when it came to light that many of its prominent members had worked for the Stasi. With so many leading figures either having co-operated with state organs themselves or having relied on others to do so on their behalf, the result of the debate within the church on how to evaluate Stolpe's Stasi connections was really a foregone conclusion. In October 1992, a declaration was drawn up by the Protestant church of Berlin-Brandenburg, stating that 'Manfred Stolpe may have periodically gone a step too far' but that ultimately he had been 'a man of the church and not of the MfS' (I-21). In 1995 the Protestant Church of Germany released a similar statement, announcing that although Stolpe had periodically overstepped the mark in his dealings with the Stasi, no disciplinary measures were to be taken against him:

> He carried out these dialogues as a representative of the church. He did not go over to the other side. In the course of and above and beyond his professional duties he showed extraordinary commitment in successfully dealing with varied church and humanitarian concerns (I-24).

In the course of investigations into Manfred Stolpe's Stasi past, several leading political figures from the FRG came before the Committee and spoke out in his defence. Former Chancellor Helmut Schmidt said of his conversations with Manfred Stolpe: 'I simply didn't say anything which I did not want to go any further' (F-2, I, 187). Schmidt went on to say that, since he had explicitly asked Stolpe to convey information to leading Party members in the East, it would be absurd to reproach him for having done so (ibid.). The former Foreign Minister, Hans-Dietrich Genscher, also spoke out in Stolpe's defence: 'It wasn't just that I took into account that the details of these conversations would be relayed by those taking part in them to the powers that be in the GDR, but I actually wanted this to happen' (ibid. I, p. 189). Statements such as these from prominent figures brought to light the issue of the West's own complicity with the system in force in the GDR. Leading politicians from the West had welcomed the contact which they were able to establish through Manfred Stolpe, and had gladly used him as a go-between. Stolpe was, of course, only able to fulfil this role precisely because he was prepared to have dealings with those in power in the GDR, something his more idealistic contemporaries were less willing to do. After the official recognition of the GDR by the FRG and the gradual relaxing of the Cold War mentality between the two Germanys, a figure like Stolpe had provided a valuable means of realising dialogue between political adversaries. If Stolpe was to be condemned for the role he had played, then so too must those in the West who had used him to achieve their own ends, by taking into account, and indeed actively welcoming the fact that here was a man who had close links to those in power in the GDR.

It was not, of course, only in former West Germany that Stolpe found wide-spread support, but also in the five new federal states of united Germany. The journalist Robert Leicht aptly summed up the reasons as to why this should be the case:

> At the end of the day Manfred Stolpe only benefited from the debate over his problematic past, above all because then as now he actually only ever was a controversial negotiator and not a traitor. And many people identify with him in as much as he represents the 'historical compromise' made to survive in the GDR – those who did resist the regime, but not to extremes, and those who conformed to it, but not on every single count (I-88).

It was only a small minority of East Germans who did not fit into one of the two groups defined above. Stolpe was, therefore, a comfortable figure to identify with. His position in the GDR had not involved policy making, and in this sense he was freed from any direct responsibility for the injustices perpetrated there. Yet Stolpe had not resisted the system in the way in which prominent dissidents had done. He had presumed that the GDR would exist beyond his lifetime, a point he makes repeatedly in

Schwieriger Aufbruch, and had worked with and not against the system in order to achieve his aims:

> The ambivalent nature of post-Stalinist entanglement, which has been illuminated by the Stolpe case and of which we in the West have only a vague understanding, makes it even more difficult to come to any moral judgement on individual cases.
>
> (Jürgen Habermas, I-80, p. 83)

It was those who initially might have been presumed to be political adversaries, that is representatives of the citizens' rights movement of the former GDR, and members of Helmut Kohl's Christian Democratic Union (CDU), who met on common ground in their wish to see Stolpe forced into resignation. These two groups were often united on the question of how various aspects of the Stasi legacy should be confronted, and some years after unification seven former representatives of the citizens' rights movement, among them Günter Nooke and Vera Lengsfeld (formerly Wollenberger), caused a sensation when they did in fact join the CDU (I-95).

In contrast to those who had held dissident status in the GDR, the interest of the population at large in the lengthy debate surrounding Stolpe's Stasi connections gradually began to wane. A survey carried out in late 1992 found that 80 per cent of those questioned wished an end to the Stolpe debate (I-9). The work of the Stolpe Committee carried on for a year and a half after this survey, but the initial positions of those active on it remained unchanged. Leading representatives of the citizens' rights groups refused in the end to come before the committee, wishing by their refusal to protest at the fact that they had been invited to give testimony at such a late stage in the overall proceedings (I-22). Their testimonies may well, as they claimed, have had little impact at this late stage, but their protest also proved futile, in that its symbolic nature seemed merely to support Stolpe's previous claim that the difference between himself and Bärbel Bohley was that whereas he was a pragmatist, Bohley was an fundamentalist (I-81, p. 3).

The work of the Stolpe Committee, whose final report was published in June 1994, had been highly topical and controversial. The core problem in bringing the Stolpe debate to any sort of satisfying conclusion was that which is encountered in any case where someone's previous Stasi contacts are examined; namely that there is no consensus on the question of what exactly makes this contact a punishable offence in unified Germany. The Committee spent much time and effort examining the details of Stolpe's Stasi contacts, notably those surrounding the awarding of the infamous service medal, and the question of whether or not he had been aware that he had been referred to by the cover name of 'Sekretär'. Throughout these deliberations, Stolpe quite simply refused to resign his political mandate and in the absence of the ultimate proof of a written commitment, and with numerous statements of support from prominent politicians and theologians, he was able to remain in office. There is really no doubt that, as far as the Stasi was concerned, Manfred Stolpe was an unofficial employee, in that he met with Stasi officers regularly and secretly, and supplied them with information. Had a written commitment been found in the course of the investigation, Stolpe would probably have been under considerably more pressure to resign. This is confirmed by the wording of the Committee's final report, which states that, since there was no proof that Stolpe knew that he had been registered under the name 'Sekretär', or that he had ever explicitly committed himself to work as an informer, he had been 'an equal partner in negotiations with them' (F-2, I, 165). Yet this statement ignores evidence from the files. The fact that no document was found in which Stolpe committed himself in writing in effect proved nothing. Stasi guidelines suggest that it was often the case that individuals such as Stolpe were not asked to make a written commitment:

> A systematic and goal-oriented approach to working with members of the intelligentsia and particularly with church dignitaries should lead to an increase of trust of the MfS on their part and to the MfS obtaining important and valuable information from them.
>
> The end result of constant ideological influence should be the creation of a close working relationship, with the result that in special cases a written declaration of commitment may even be foregone, if without this written commitment the goal can be more easily attained, i.e., that by working together a tight bond is formed (J-62, p. 212).

Despite this evidence from Stasi documentation, the Stolpe Committee placed much importance on details such as the existence of a material commitment, never really scratching the surface of the issues at hand to discuss how, in the historical context of the GDR, such contacts to state organs should be evaluated. The discussion could potentially have been significantly more enlightening if it had been accepted from the outset that Stolpe had to all intents and purposes been a bona fide unofficial employee. The question of whether he had compromised himself and others to too great an extent in order to achieve his aims could then have been examined in detail. Robert Leicht suggested that the avoidance of the real issues involved was partly due to the stance which Stolpe's opponents adopted from the outset:

> The most exciting thing about the Stolpe case was the question of political ethos it illuminated: In what relationship did the deeply questionable contacts to the State Security Service stand to the humanitarian, political and ecclesiastical results achieved through them? However, it was precisely this discussion which was never allowed to develop, because Stolpe's strongest critics abhorred the mere thought of a legitimate relationship between means and purpose – and to be on the safe side many of his supporters thus came out in blanket defence of his actions. [. . .] The avoidance of the real questions worked in Stolpe's favour and against his opponents (I-87).

It was, however, not only Stolpe's opponents who ensured that the most potentially fruitful issues of this debate were neglected. The political order of the day dictated that if Stolpe were to be shown to have known that he was registered as 'Sekretär', then he would have been under considerable pressure to resign. As a result, this became the principal question with which the committee busied itself. It was extremely difficult to establish the exact details of events which lay so far in the past, and contradictions and ambivalence were the only result of attempts to do so. Such was the inconclusive nature of proceedings that Joachim Nawrocki remarked at the end of the Committee's twenty-fifth sitting: 'It might all have happened sort of this way or that way – but then again it might not have done' (I-86). Stolpe had in fact predicted the uncertainty and ambiguity which would dominate the work of the Committee later set up to investigate his Stasi connections. In his book, he stated that in the frequent conversations he had with Stasi officers, it was possible that what he had said had not always been reported in the way in which he had meant it, and that controversial statements he had actually made might well have been left out of the subsequent reports (J-91, pp. 127, 139). Stolpe seems thus to have anticipated or known that he was on record as an unofficial employee and trivialised this fact in advance: 'Possibly the State Security Service referred to people as employees in their internal reports without their knowledge' (ibid. p. 128).

In the end, the Stolpe Committee accepted the version of events which Stolpe presented, that the pact he had made with those in power in the

SED state was one made of necessity and was justifiable. Since Stolpe's position was one with which many identified, if he were judged to have acted in a morally justifiable manner, then by default so too had the vast majority of East Germans under the dictatorship. In his book, Stolpe does indeed reinforce the concept of a common identity for East Germans, attributing collective responsibility for the past: 'At the end of the day everyone who remained there, worked and paid taxes supported the system, whether he wanted to or not' (J-91, p. 12).

The ramifications of the Stolpe debate were immense and the Brandenburg state government decided on the basis of the Stolpe Committee's conclusions that merely asserting that someone had worked for the Stasi was not sufficient information to pass judgement, and further: 'No one should be denied the chance of personal development and the desire to redirect their life' (H-2; F-15, pp. 5–6). That it is widely accepted that the course of action which Stolpe took was justified is reflected in the findings of an extensive survey carried out into East and West Germans' views on various aspects of the confrontation with the Stasi legacy. The study found that only just under one quarter of both East and West Germans questioned considered that Stolpe had compromised himself to too great an extent in order to achieve his aims (F-12).

The Stolpe debate also accented an issue which had begun to be the cause of much controversy at the time when the Committee took up its work, that is the role which the BStU was to play in the confrontation with the cumbersome legacy. Arnold Vaatz, then Environmental Minister for Saxony, said that such was the significance of the Stolpe case, that if his name were to be cleared then everyone who had been dismissed on the grounds of having been a Stasi informer would have to be reinstated and the BStU would have to be closed (I-40, p. 34). The Stolpe debate certainly did at times seem almost like a personal contest between BStU head, Joachim Gauck, and Stolpe. It appeared as though only one of the two would emerge triumphant at the end of a battle which actually reached the courts on several occasions. Stolpe took Gauck to court after the latter had claimed in an interview that it was only in the state of Brandenburg that the evidence which had been brought against Manfred Stolpe would be regarded as insufficient to force his resignation. The courts ruled that this was a value judgement which Gauck was not entitled to make in his role as Federal Commissioner of the Stasi files. Gauck's assigned task, he was reminded, was to provide the Stolpe Committee with any information it required and not to evaluate this material (J-1). In another court case, Stolpe was granted access to what was termed a 'special file' containing material relating to his person, but was not, as he had originally requested, allowed to have the entire 178 kilometres of files searched in order to have a dossier compiled with the results (I-17). The writer, Herta Müller, described Gauck's problem in this battle as follows: 'Many people identify with Stolpe, but only a few with Gauck. And now those loyal to him act as though it were Gauck and not Stolpe who made the Stasi sinister' (I-83, p. 50). In the end, both parties won and lost. Stolpe's name was officially cleared, but as long as the BStU continues to exist there is a chance that new, potentially incriminating material will be found and that the case could be re-opened. For its part, the BStU continues to be inundated with applications from the private and public sector to view the files, and in October 1995 Gauck was confirmed in his post as Federal Commissioner for a second five-year term. In the end, however, the Stolpe Committee chose to attribute just as much credibility to the testimonies of former Stasi officers as to the material which was compiled by the BStU (F-2, I, pp. 27–30).

GREGOR GYSI: A SPECIAL CASE?

The debate surrounding the alleged Stasi career of PDS golden boy Gregor Gysi bore many similarities to the Manfred Stolpe affair. The budding post-unification political career of the former lawyer began to be endangered when, after viewing their Stasi files, a number of those who had been represented by Gysi in the GDR claimed that the evidence they found in these documents proved beyond doubt that he had abused his position of trust to betray confidential information to the Stasi (I-52). In response to these allegations, Gysi claimed time and time again: 'I never directly and consciously gave information to the State Security Service' (I-54, p. 49). Although information seeming to stem from Gysi is found under the code names 'Gregor' and 'Notar' in the files, it appears that Gysi, possibly as a result of his social standing, was not considered a typical unofficial employee, but rather a 'special case' (I-70). No formal file or statement of written commitment could be uncovered for Gysi, leading the BStU to conclude: 'It is clear that the MfS did not organise its dealings with Gysi in the same way as those with a regular unofficial employee' (I-70).

Since Gysi was even less willing than Stolpe to engage in dialogue concerning his dealings with the Stasi, any attempt to initiate debate proved futile, and the issue soon deteriorated into an at times petty battle between Gysi and a number of former citizens' rights campaigners, principally Katja Havemann, the last wife of prominent dissident, Robert Havemann, who claimed that Gysi had abused her husband's trust, and Bärbel Bohley, who was taken to court on a number of occasions over the question of whether she was permitted to refer to Gysi as a Stasi snoop (I-4; I-69). Bohley continued to refer to Gysi in this way even after she had been threatened with a substantial fine for doing so, defiantly declaring: 'I'm not going to pay anything for any informer, I'd rather go to prison' (I-25).

A wide range of public personalities began to take sides in the Gysi issue, notably, and predictably, Gysi's political adversaries in the CDU (I-5). Signed declarations were drawn up for and against Gysi, with thirty opponents claiming in one such statement: 'Through his function as a lawyer Gregor Gysi carved himself one of the biggest careers in the system of lies, spying and injustice in force in the GDR' (I-89). A public declaration, signed by the likes of Stefan Heym, Heiner Müller and even various politicians from elsewhere in Europe, argued on the contrary: 'The fact that the accused is forced to prove his innocence rather than having his guilt ascertained is a reversal of the burden of proof and a serious violation of democratic legal principles' (I-26). Statements such as these did nothing to encourage any form of open dialogue. Indeed, the likelihood of this ever being realised had become even more remote after Gysi, in May 1995, made a public statement that, unless new incriminating evidence were produced, he was not prepared to enter into any further debate concerning his Stasi connections: 'I am no longer prepared to take part in the futile ride on the worn-out carousel' (I-32). Although in 1998 the Immunity Committee of the German parliament concluded that, despite his claims to the contrary, Gysi had knowingly supplied the Stasi with information, the fact that no standard statement of written commitment has been or is ever likely to be found, may once again, as in the Stolpe debate, prove decisive. Unless absolute proof can be uncovered that he willingly and consciously gave information on his clients to the Stasi, Gysi's charisma and charm will continue to ensure that the widespread support he has in the former GDR is sufficient to let him remain a force to be reckoned with in the political or, indeed, in any other arena of post-unification Germany.

7

JUSTICE AND THE LAW

> One cannot expect a revolution to adhere to the law. At the same time a revolution which to some extent took place holding a candle in its hand cannot demand that the legal organs make up for what the revolutionaries neglected to do or think that they neglected to do (I-14, p. 126).

After he had been given a two-year suspended sentence for his role in the death of Chris Gueffroy (the last person to be killed while trying to flee the GDR) Andreas Kühnpast, one of the four border-guards on trial, said of the judgement: 'It was not about upholding the legal principles of a democracy but was completely arbitrary' (I-8). This first in a series of border-guard trials was representative of much of the legal reckoning with the GDR legacy, in that it highlighted some of the key difficulties and points of contention involved in such an undertaking. The border-guards had, by firing the fatal shots, been the most directly responsible for the death of the young Gueffroy, yet they were at the very bottom of the power hierarchy and were not responsible for the order to shoot anyone who attempted to cross into the FRG. The courts had to decide if the argumentation used in the border-guards' defence, that they had merely been following orders, was acceptable. This was for many an uncomfortably familiar argument in the German context, and Ralf Giordano argued that it was time that the Germans began to face up to their responsibility, not just for giving, but also for following orders (cited in J-45, p. 180). Yet any severe punishment of these foot soldiers would have seemed inappropriate when those who had been responsible for the order to shoot were not, at least at this point, being brought to trial. Bringing a case to bear on those higher up the power hierarchy was a considerably more lengthy and complicated process, and it was not until 1996 that the trial against six leading Party members began for their part in the deaths at the German–German border.

These proceedings tend to be characterised by a series of delays and interruptions, caused either by the waning health of the accused or by formal objections raised on various formalities.

The chief legal difficulty in dealings with crimes committed in the GDR is the principle of *nulla poena sine lege*, Article 103 (2) of the German constitution: 'A crime can only be punished if it was declared punishable by law before it was committed.' This principle has been contested on many occasions since 1945, and Giordano argues that this clause, by decreeing that 'law = justice', effectively means that if Hitler had created legislation for genocide then no one could have been tried for their role in carrying out the Final Solution (I-66). In order for the state of law to remain credible, however, it has to be seen to adhere to the legal principles which it has defined, and the idea that this clause could be nullified in the legal reckoning with the GDR past was never really given serious consideration. Andreas Zielcke commented as follows on the difficulties involved: 'The paradox of the democratic legal system lies in the fact that it is unable to confront a dictatorship in its courts of law' (I-46, p. 79).

Addressing the difficulties of the legal confrontation with the GDR past, the then Foreign Minister Klaus Kinkel stressed that, in confronting the crimes of the SED state, it was not a question of imposing some sort of victor's justice: 'It is simply about justice. Guilt, however, has to be proven on a concrete and individual basis' (J-40, p. 6). Establishing individual guilt is, however, an extremely complex legal problem and Kinkel admitted that this was what made the trials so difficult (ibid.). One consequence of the legal difficulties in bringing such cases to court, as the journalist Rainer Frenkl observed, was that in the trials against leading Party members, the gap between the actual political guilt and the charges brought could not have been more crass (I-84). In an often farcical trial Erich Mielke, for example, initially stood accused of the murder of two policemen in the 1930s, and not for any injustices he was responsible for as the head of the Stasi. Another of the most powerful men in the GDR, Markus Wolf, was first sentenced in December 1993 to six years imprisonment for his role as head of foreign espionage. At the time, Wolf declared: 'I am to be condemned for the fact that the GDR existed for forty years, something which according to the legal and political understanding of those who passed judgement should never have been allowed to happen' (F-6, p. 34). In 1995, this verdict was declared invalid and overturned. Wolf could only have been legally punished if he had worked for a foreign power. Since he had carried out his duties as a GDR citizen, and from the territory of the GDR, it was decreed that he was free from guilt in a legal sense.

In general, the higher up the power hierarchy an individual had been, the more difficult it proved to bring a case to bear. Even former head of state, Erich Honecker, who was eventually freed from detainment on the grounds of ill-health, maintained that he considered himself 'free from any guilt from a legal point of view' (I-77). Many former Stasi victims were disappointed to discover that the criminal justice system would not necessarily guarantee justice for the crimes which had been committed in the dictatorship. Marion Gräfin-Dönhoff denounced Bärbel Bohley's now infamous comment that the citizens of the GDR had hoped for justice and had got the criminal justice system, as a 'terrible sentence', accusing Bohley of confusing justice with revenge (I-92). It was a bitter discovery not only for Bohley, but for many of those who had suffered injustices in the GDR that, since the FRG's criminal justice system was based on the principle that the accused was innocent until proven guilty, it would offer just as much protection to those who had served the Stasi as to those who had suffered at its hands. The Neues Forum in Halle, for example, was taken to court after it made allegedly anonymously-donated lists of former Stasi employees available for public consultation. Although checks at the BStU indicated that most of the people on the lists had in fact actually worked for the Stasi on an official or unofficial basis, the courts ruled that the individual rights of those concerned outweighed the right of the public to this information (I-27). Katrin Eigenfeld of the Neues Forum argued that the publishing of the lists had been entirely successful as it had resulted in a 'psychological cleansing' in the town (F-13, p. 160). This may well have been the case for many of those concerned, but those who were not quite as enamoured with the action taken were entitled to make use of the principles of the criminal justice system in what proved to be a run of costly court cases for the Neues Forum.

Wolf Biermann sees much of the frustration with the limitations of the criminal justice system as resulting from the fact that the public demonstrations of 1989 involved 'too little barbaric substance, too little organised foresight, yes, and too little blind anger' (I-44, p. 83). The presence of a little more blind anger could, he suggested, have been cathartic for the East German population, allowing them to vent their aggressions and to feel that justice had in some way been done. This was, however, not to be. Without a single death and very little bloodshed the GDR ceased to be and merged with the FRG. The fact that these events took place so peacefully and without any lynch justice meant that there remained a lot of guilt which had not in any way been seen to be atoned. Many placed their hopes in the criminal justice system, presuming that it would be capable of carrying out this task, and were disillusioned to discover that the legal system and a higher notion of justice were two quite separate constructs, one of which was concrete, and one abstract. In a discussion of the concepts of justice and law, Derrida argues that the English phrase 'to enforce the law' is useful, since it serves as a reminder that the law is always something which is imposed by force. He continues: 'Force on its own without justice is tyrannical. Justice with no force behind it is not recognised, because there are always those who will try to abuse it' (J-19, p. 11). The point being made here is precisely that which was disregarded by those who had hoped that justice and the law were one and the same.

* * *

When the Stasi Document Law came into force in late December 1991 it allowed full implementation of the ruling in the Unification Treaty which stated that civil servants found to have worked for the Stasi could be dismissed (G-1). For those active in the public sector who still lived with the secret of having been an informer, this law meant that their days in employment were potentially numbered. Within the first three years of the law coming into existence, well over one million applications had been lodged from employers in the public sector wishing to discover if their employees had worked for the Stasi (F-17, p. 111). For the vast majority of those screened in this way the answer is negative, since, after all, it was only a small minority of the East German population which was active as informers. Of 20,000 teachers screened in the Berlin area, for example, 4.5 per cent were found to have had such connections to the Stasi (ibid. pp. 7–8).

Comparing the way in which former Secret Service employees were being treated in Germany with the Czech Republic, Tina Rosenberg concluded that the German approach was fairer, since individuals are not necessarily dismissed if they are discovered to have worked for the Stasi (J-73, p. 321). The German system, however, is only potentially fairer. In practice, comparable cases are often treated inconsistently within and between states. Reflecting on these discrepancies, Rosenberg does comment on the absurdity, as she puts it, that 'Manfred Stolpe can be governor of Brandenburg, but [because of his previous Stasi connections] he could not drive a tram in Saxony' (J-73, p. 324). The German system therefore allows for, but does not demand a differentiated treatment of individual cases. There are no set rules as to what constitutes sufficient grounds for dismissal, and some decisions are thus bound to be undifferentiated. There have, indeed, been many reports of inconsistencies in the screening of civil servants (I-18; I-49). These arose partly because each committee responsible for examining individual cases set its own criteria for deciding whether the person concerned should be allowed to remain in employment. Werner Fischer, who was involved in the screening of public service employees in Berlin, reported that the committee took the length of service to the Stasi into account, but that all those who were still active in the autumn of 1989 were automatically dismissed (I-43, p. 68). Since there are bound to be crass differences in the degree of involvement and in the resulting culpability of all those who were still active as informers in 1989, the decision to dismiss all of this group is potentially unfair to those whose co-operation may have been minimal. Legislation has, indeed, already been passed meaning that since August 1998, the BStU is no longer obliged to disclose information concerning informers whose career with the Stasi came to an end before 31 December 1975 (I-60). Furthermore, even if individuals were involved with the Stasi after 1976, information does not have to be released to an employer or potential employer if it is decided that the extent of compliance was minimal. There are, however, certain exceptions to this ruling. Information concerning Members of Parliament will, for example, still be released. For many of those who have been out of work for a period of years as a result of having been a Stasi informer, it will be no easy task to find employment again, even after such a change in legislation. In addition, such an alteration is likely to only offer further incentive for those whose Stasi connections have not yet come to light to continue to remain silent about this aspect of their biography. It is, however, only a small minority even of those found to have held contacts to the Stasi who actually do lose their jobs. Of the 4.5 per cent of teachers in the Berlin area found to have worked for the Stasi, a mere 0.9 per cent was eventually dismissed after the cases had been reviewed (F-17, pp. 7–8). Furthermore, some of this small number who are dismissed are able to contest this decision on the basis of procedural errors and have to be subsequently reinstated.

* * *

A recurring problem in the debate concerning the legal reckoning with the GDR past is the clear confusion in some cases of legal and moral issues. This confounding of moral and legal guilt is particularly evident in dealings with the questionnaire about possible Stasi connections which was given to public service employees from the GDR. Many who had worked as informers did not admit to this fact on the questionnaire. The fact that they had been untruthful was sometimes used as a further reproach when their Stasi past eventually did come to light. 'Falke' was informed in the letter announcing his dismissal that if he had been honest about his Stasi past in the first place he would never have been appointed to his promoted position in the police force and that 'in addition, by keeping quiet about the work for the Ministry of State Security you have destroyed the relationship between yourself and your employer' (B-4). Since there were no legal consequences of lying on the questionnaire, there was only a moral incentive to tell the truth. 'Falke' would have lost his job even if he had taken the more morally admirable stance of admitting to his Stasi contacts. He was, nevertheless, reproached for not having done so as though this morally more correct behaviour could actually have influenced the decision to sack him. Telling the truth about having worked for the Stasi only meant that informers were likely to be dismissed sooner. Lying generally led to being able to remain in employment longer, but could result in a moral reproach when the truth was revealed. The questionnaires were thus merely a pseudo-legal way of confronting the Stasi legacy, leading Friedrich Schorlemmer to remark: 'The nature of the questionnaires makes me feel solidarity with those for whom I previously had no respect at all' (J-82, p. 234).

* * *

The role of the BStU has also been the subject of heated debate in the legal confrontation with the Stasi legacy. The writer Stefan Heym spoke out in criticism of the BStU, claiming that united Germany was ruled by it and by the *Treuhand*, the much-disputed body set up to administer the sale of GDR state properties. Between them, he argued, these two government bodies had more power than the Politburo in deciding individual fates, by producing information which:

> the rest of humanity is just supposed to accept without question – and which is used to pass judgement on and get rid of specific individuals, who are not even given the chance to take a look at the alleged evidence of their guilt [the Stasi files] or defend themselves. It wasn't even this bad in the inquisition – at least then those who survived the torture were forgiven. And at least people were given a hearing with the infamous Senator McCarthy (J-36, p. 73).

Heym is certainly not alone in his disapproval and distrust of the BStU. During the debate concerning the creation of the Stasi Document Law, Jürgen Fuchs wondered, for example, whether it would be at all possible for a government body to deal with all the 'suffering' and the 'humiliation' contained in the Stasi files (F-16, p. 396). Fuchs believed that the answer to this question was negative and argued that the files should be kept where they were found and administered 'without all that terrible rhetoric found in such institutions' (ibid.). It was decided, however, that the only way to ensure that those who had suffered most would be protected from being done a second injustice was to allow the files to be administered by such an institution who could meticulously control who obtained access and under what conditions to the very intimate, hurtful, and potentially exploitable personal information which makes up a substantial part of the Stasi's documental legacy. The fact that the BStU is now a government body acting within the constraints of the Stasi Document Law is often ignored. At times, one might be led to think that it was all the invention of one man, Joachim Gauck. The BStU is more commonly referred to as the Gauck Office, and the process of screening public service employees is even sometimes popularly referred to as 'gaucking'. Gauck the person is then often strongly identified with the institution of which he is in charge. This has been the case from the BStU's early days and in 1991, the Humanitarian Union went back on its decision to award Gauck an honour as it was felt that to do so would be an indication of approval of dealings with the Stasi legacy (I-6; G-2). Another example of such thinking is seen when Lesley Bodi comments that 'Gauck and his supporters have tended to side with the victims and not the culprits' (J-12, p. 15).

There is no doubt that, as head of the BStU, Joachim Gauck does agitate politically, but his actions are always bound by a law created and approved by the German parliament, a law which should only ever be seen as one facet of the societal confrontation with the Stasi legacy, since in the words of Ralf Giordano: 'The legal system can only partly address the confrontation with the past. This confrontation is to a much greater extent a matter of individual or personal cleansing and has nothing to do with penitentiaries and prisons' (J-92, pp. 182–3).

Since German unification in 1990, there have been many calls for an amnesty for former Stasi employees (see I-51; I-91; J-21). These are often motivated by the recognition of the immense difficulties involved in dealing with the crimes of the GDR within the legal system. The low number of cases reaching the courts is also partly due to the fact that so few victims of the Stasi are coming forward to accuse their former tormentors, even when it would be feasible to bring a legal charge. In one notable case, a man was awarded a substantial sum of money when he took his nephew to court for having informed the GDR authorities of his uncle's plans to flee to the West. The denunciation had resulted in the uncle receiving a three year prison sentence and subsequent ban from working in his trade (I-71). Many other Stasi victims decide, however, against taking legal action. Even Bärbel Bohley admitted that she had not taken this step, but that she would not like to have this right taken from her, arguing that an amnesty would mean that the state was effectively saying to its citizens: 'Look at your files, but don't bother the courts' (I-55, p. 94). Bohley also argued that since many had still to view their files, an amnesty would mean that the right to bring their oppressors to court would be taken from some Stasi victims before they had been given the chance to exercise it (ibid.).

Even if more will were there, it would be extremely difficult to bring many Stasi informers to court, since their primary guilt lies most often in the fact that they abused the trust of others. This is a moral guilt which cannot clearly be defined or punished within the criminal justice system. The confrontation with this guilt cannot be decreed from above and can only take place on an interpersonal level. Difficulties in realising such interpersonal contacts lie partly in the fact that the legal context for confronting the Stasi legacy does exist. Since admitting to having worked for the Stasi can result in dismissal, these immediate material concerns tend to overshadow the consideration of moral issues for informers. Attempts in the immediate post-Wende period to establish a forum for open discussion between former Stasi workers and those who were spied upon were thus ultimately doomed, and although a so-called Forum for Clarification and Renewal was founded, it was largely unsuccessful. The forum's aims were stated as follows:

> To engage unbiased experts and to put together an independent panel to lead proceedings. Instead of passing a legal judgement the aim should be to ascertain, publicly document and evaluate the circumstances, events and chains of responsibility which resulted in injustice being carried out (F-9, p. 6).

Apart from the clear difficulties in deciding who exactly these 'unbiased experts' were to be, it is difficult to imagine how this 'independent panel' could have come to its conclusions without making value judgements on the past actions of individual actors. There are, however, clearly issues of moral guilt which cannot be dealt with within the criminal justice system. It is to this equally problematic personal and interpersonal confrontation with the Stasi legacy which the following chapters will now turn.

8

THE GUILT CONTINUUM

Defining degrees of conformity and resistance

The brunt of the anger displayed when Stasi premises were stormed and occupied in late 1989 and early 1990 often fell on those at the very bottom of the hierarchy of power, on the Stasi's secret helpers, the informers. Many of the 174,000 unofficial employees registered active in 1989, and of the many others who had worked in this capacity in the past, were not known as such to even close friends and relatives. The most extreme example of such a case was that concerning Vera Wollenberger (now Lengsfeld), who discovered that her husband Knud had been informing on her under the cover name of 'Donald' for many years. There was, at least initially, a period of uncertainty in certain interpersonal relationships when it seemed that the mysterious figure of the informer was 'everywhere and nowhere, it might have been almost anyone and in the end it was no-one' (J-102, p. 135). Clarifying who had or had not worked as a Stasi informer and putting an end to mass, often erroneous, speculation was considerably more difficult before the Stasi Document Law came into force at the end of 1991. Very few informers were prepared to come forward and admit to what they had done. Bärbel Bohley bemoaned, for example, the fact that, of over 50 informers reporting on her, not one approached her and confessed (I-1). Bohley had to wait until she was granted access to her Stasi file before she could establish with certainty exactly who had been reporting on her activities.

Bärbel Bohley may have been surprised at the extent and form of the observation of her public and private life but she, as someone the Stasi had classifed a dissident, could be sure that her activities had been closely monitored. Others did not have this certainty, yet had lived their lives in the belief that their words and actions could potentially be recorded at any time. As a result, many had to some extent lived as though they were being observed, effectively assuming a role as a victim of Stasi surveillance, without actually knowing that this was the case:

> The Stasi was present during every discussion like the monster in a horror film. It destroyed the trust of the people who lived in its state and played a major role in its downfall. The Stasi spied on people and pursued them. And millions of people felt that they were being spied upon and pursued. Both parties together formed a horror partnership of the pursuer and the pursued, of the perpetrator and the real or presumed victim (J-101, p. 11).

Many of these 'presumed victims' were, in accordance with the Focusing Principle, not actually under observation at all. In the Leipzig area, 500 of 670 OPK underway in 1989 concerned individuals involved in the church, in cultural groups, or in opposition movements, and only 23 OV were in operation outside these three areas (F-13, p. 32). The Focusing Principle was, however, not always adhered to, particularly it seems in the early years. Speaking in 1953, the then Secretary of State for State Security, Ernst Wollweber, complained:

> The weakness of the informer network lies above all in the fact that it is spread equally over all areas and does not take the concentration of fascist and other enemy elements in the key industries and institutions into account (F-5, I, p. 59).

This and later evidence suggests that significant numbers of informers were not employed on the basis of the Focusing Principle at all, but rather because they were loyal citizens who proved relatively easy to recruit and subsequently manage. Nevertheless, there was still a marked tendency to concentrate the network of observation in the three groups named above, with the result that in sections of society outside these groups there were many 'presumed victims'. Hence, a type of big brother system functioned in the minds of the East German population which did not reflect the reality of the situation. The writer Jurek Becker believed that this phenomenon of perceived observation, resulting to a certain extent in many people imposing a form of self-censorship, was a major contributory factor in the Stasi's success:

> One of the Stasi's greatest strengths lay in the fact that one often presumed its representatives to be present when in reality this wasn't the case. Many telephone conversations only took place for the benefit of the person listening in. Letters contained empty phrases which were not meant for the person they were addressed to but for the person monitoring them, and at public gatherings

> (everyone's life was full of public gatherings) you made even yourself sick with your applause at certain points. One doesn't therefore have to look for long for the reasons behind the anger that is now being unloaded on the cursed Stasi (J-33, p. 77).

The fact that many more people presumed themselves observed than was actually the case is reflected in the finding that over 40 per cent of those who apply to the BStU to see their Stasi file have to be told that no such file exists (F-8, p. 52). Some of this number are extremely reluctant to believe that this is the case and apply again in the belief that the BStU has not been thorough enough in the search for material (ibid.). It is possible that the files held on a proportion of these individuals were partially or wholly destroyed in the Stasi's hurried attempts to get rid of potentially explosive material in its dying days. Most of these non-Stasi-victims are, however, faced with the probability that their activities within the GDR were simply not considered enough of a threat to warrant observation and, if they choose to confront this fact, are forced to reflect more closely on what role they actually did play, if not that of a bona fide victim. Such a confrontation with the past requires a great deal of potentially unpleasant soul searching, and Lutz Rathenow suggests therefore that 'File Envy' will become a psychological phenomenon of the future (J-69, p. 64). Even some of those who stormed Stasi headquarters crying, 'I want my file' have since discovered that no such file exists. Rathenow believes that these and other potential sufferers from File Envy would rather forget the past than confront it: 'In the long term it is not the perpetrators who endanger a true confrontation with the past, but those who can hardly bear not to have been Stasi victims' (ibid.).

The realisation that there were very many more supposed rather than genuine targets of direct observation forces a re-evaluation of personal and collective history. If this large group of non-victims did not behave in such a way as to warrant Stasi observation, yet felt themselves to be opposed to the state to the extent that they suspected a file might have been held on them, how then can their behaviour pattern be best described?

Various analyses of the average citizen's behaviour in the GDR have been proposed since 1989. Wolf Biermann argued that 'the deceived people were themselves deceivers. For years they pulled the wool over their rulers' eyes with all the celebration parades and the torch-lit marches' (I-78, p. 73). Maaz, on the contrary, argues that the East German psyche was characterised by a split personality (J-54, p. 76). This split in personality enabled East Germans to betray their private convictions in public, and explains why, for example, well over 90 per cent of the population went along with the farcical pretence of democratic elections. Maaz argues that many GDR citizens simply did not feel what they saw or heard. Had they done so, they would have had to confront their public conformity to a system about which they privately harboured grave doubts (ibid. p. 77). Psychologist Harry Schröder, by comparison, divides East Germans into three groups: standard conformists; non- or anti-conformists; and opportunistic conformists (J-83, pp. 166–7; J-85). Standard conformists were individuals who, at least initially, believed in the system and found justification for their actions as representatives of it. The number of such individuals decreased throughout the GDR's existence, but some who had become disillusioned worked hard to continue convincing themselves of their stance, motivated by their previous commitment and by the desire to preserve the way of life to which they had become accustomed. Only a small percentage of East Germans belonged to the second group of non- or rather anti-conformists. These were individuals who spoke out or took decisive critical action against the status quo. Most East Germans fell into the third group of opportunistic conformists, defined by Schröder as follows:

> They were quite genuinely ruled by circumstances. They adapted to the status quo and by doing so ensured its continued existence. They identified less and less with the dominating ideology. [. . .] They strove to create and exploit windows of opportunity, to keep on a straight line, to protect others and to fight injustice. Many East Germans stress this stance today, to avoid being accused of having simply changed their allegiance overnight – and most do, at least in some respects, actually have a case to make (J-83, p. 167).

The majority had, according to Schröder, simply learned to live with the existing power structures and to use them to their own advantage. Although, as Jens Reich puts it, many East Germans viewed the GDR with an 'ironic distance' and may even have periodically engaged in acts of non-conformity, their general behavioural stance was one of opportunism (I-82). This interpretation suggests that the average East German was very much aware of the degree of disparity between public conformity and private conviction, rather than that these seemingly contradictory behaviours resulted from some kind of schizophrenic or split personality.

Even prominent 'state enemies', who, undoubtedly, were not always willing to betray their private beliefs, were very much aware of the extent at other times of their own compliance. Jürgen Fuchs, for example, asks:

'Who didn't sometimes just keep quiet, go along with things in some way?'(J-26, p. 31). Compliance was widespread, and the day of true revolt came very late for many critical minds. The stance which Jens Reich admits to having taken was typical:

> For many years I carried on with my job, kept my mouth shut, sat in a political niche and only realised at a late date, much too late, that my role in life could not have been always to have known better but to have kept quiet about it (I-53, p. 41).

Statements such as the above underline the fact that conforming was often a conscious action which resulted in cognitive dissonance, rather than a behavioural tendency which was caused by a split in personality. Environmental campaigner Michael Beleites suggests that some form of discord was inevitable, regardless of how one behaved. Both conformity and non-conformity resulted in conflict. If East Germans behaved in a way which was at odds with their private beliefs, this resulted in inner conflict. If, on the other hand, they chose to resolve this inner conflict by acting in accordance with their true convictions, these actions led to outer conflict with the state (F-14, p. 85). The majority of East Germans opted during most of the GDR's existence for the inner conflict, choosing to live with the resultant cognitive dissonance rather than with the undoubtedly more unpredictable outer conflict of dealing with the potential wrath of the state for engaging in non-conformist activities. Jurek Becker believed that the government of the GDR was thus able to consider itself lucky since 'it had to do with a population which readily subordinated itself, with citizens whose main act of opposition consisted of getting annoyed' (J-33, p. 76).

* * *

> There are real perpetrators and real victims, guilty ones and innocent ones and then in between the many others, we – who lived there, busy getting by, more or less decent, more or less clever, more or less cowardly or brave (Wolfgang Thierse, I-75, p. 33).

Clearly not all East Germans can be characterised as falling into the group of opportunistic conformists described above. There were certainly 'real perpetrators' and 'real victims', yet defining these groups is no easy task. Maaz goes as far as to argue that even Stasi employees did not differ significantly from other East Germans. The inherent split in personality he detected not only allowed people to conform to a system in which they had no faith but, since the cognitive mechanism involved was one and the same, to be active as Stasi informers. Informers, Maaz proposes, were not like spies in films, who slyly become involved with particular individuals solely in order to obtain information:

> No, it was rather the case that the so-called 'information service' and normal life were one and the same thing. A double life was not even necessary and a particular disguise not even possible – for quite different reasons, quite independent of the Stasi. The Security Service simply benefited from this situation (J-55, p. 86).

Maaz thus suggests that it was merely a question of the extent to which the Stasi chose to exploit the split personality of all East Germans which determined whether or not they became informers and suggests that it is not possible to divide East German society into perpetrators and victims, since aspects of both were incorporated in every social ranking (J-54, p. 102). Although Maaz adds that the balance of the perpetrator and victim elements and therefore the level of guilt did vary considerably, his argumentation to some extent effectively frees informers from full individual responsibility for their actions, since these had been almost predetermined by virtue of being born in the GDR. One informer argues similarly that, whether one was a Stasi informer or someone who was merely tolerating the regime, the same psychological mechanisms were at work:

> For years your moral substance was worn away. Years and years. And it was the same for every last GDR citizen. For some to a greater degree, for others to a lesser. There was this double morality which began way back at school. This daily lie, which everyone participated in to some extent. [. . .] Once you learn to accept the big political lie you allow yourself little lies in other places. Unconsciously (J-71, p. 146).

Statements such as these relativise the potential guilt of the Stasi informer who, in the light of this wide-spread compliance, can no longer be set apart to the same extent. Friedrich Schorlemmer is indeed highly critical of those people who do attempt to distinguish their behaviour from that of informers. They are merely trying, he argues, to escape a confrontation with their individual responsibility for not having had the courage to oppose the system: 'What they previously lacked in courage is now surfacing as anger. [. . .] The vengeance is a variation of forty years of cowardliness which they do not dare to confront' (J-82, p. 252). Schorlemmer suggests that instead of striving to attribute guilt to particular individuals, the crimes of the past should be confronted collectively (J-81, p. 58). He believes, however, that most East Germans have no desire to engage in such an undertaking, adding, that he cannot really reproach anyone for this fact as 'that is how we were made here' (ibid. pp. 93, 106). Schorlemmer's argumentation seems inherently flawed, as he asks individuals to recognise that they are collectively responsible for the crimes of the past, yet at the same time liberates them from this responsibility by blaming the system for making them as they are.

Any attempt to determine levels of guilt is, in some ways, only further hampered by an analysis of the Stasi files. An examination of an unofficial employee's file not only reveals the extent of this informer's compliance, but also that of countless others who were not classified as such. These files, particularly the Personal Files, were only able to be compiled with the help of many others who may well have held no rank with the Stasi. Post, for example, which potential informers, informers and their immediate families received, particularly any correspondence from the FRG, was regularly scrutinised. The censoring and control of post was, indeed, widespread in the GDR, and Fricke reports that from a total of over one hundred thousand letters sent every day from the Dresden area, approximately four to five thousand were screened (J-25, p. 48).

Alongside copies and the occasional photograph of suspicious letters and packages which the informers or potential informers received, a variety of other documentation is also to be found in the Personal File. This can take the form of reports or references from the person's former school or place of work. The presence of this kind of material is evidence that high levels of co-operation existed between the Stasi and these various institutions and organisations. The relationship between the head of a school, for example, and the Stasi may never have been officially formalised, but this person may well have regularly supplied such documentation. There are also character descriptions of various individuals in the files which were supplied by members of the general public. The Stasi seems to have experienced little difficulty finding willing sources for this information. Herbert K, a former full-time Stasi informer, describes carrying out enquiries among the general public, claiming: 'On the whole the people we came across were open. [. . .] You wouldn't believe all the stuff we were told' (J-39, p. 58). One example of information having been supplied to the Stasi by members of the general public is documented in 'Reiner's' file. In order to check if 'Reiner' had been concealing the true nature of his work as a full-time informer as he had pledged to do, the Stasi made enquiries with neighbours of his who were judged to be trustworthy and loyal (C-4a, I, 69). Had the Stasi not been able to rely on fairly wide acceptance, or at the very least tolerance of control mechanisms such as these it would have been considerably more difficult to sustain the system of informers.

The unofficial employees went, of course, a step beyond this unstructured compliance with the system, and although it is possible that certain informers did not cause direct harm to others during the course of their work for the Stasi, Katrin Eigenfeld of the Neues Forum argues that one must also consider the indirect harm they caused:

> These informers determined my life, changed my life over those ten years. In one way or another – because they poisoned us with mistrust. They caused damage simply because I suspected that there could be informers in my vicinity (F-13, p. 132).

Some informers are, in fact, aware of the indirect damage which Eigenfeld describes, and 'Wolfgang' tells me how it shocked him to find out that his daughter had nightmares that she was being followed and observed by the Stasi even though this was not the case. He says that he had previously not considered this potential indirect consequence of the surveillance measures (A-7).

Even if they cannot be shown to have directly harmed others, the Stasi's method of collecting information from a number of sources and compiling it like a mosaic must be taken into account when discussing the relative guilt of informers. All informers are, furthermore, at the very least guilty of having potentially caused their fellow citizens the sort of indirect harm described above. Yet, such a broad statement is still unsatisfactory since it does not distinguish levels of guilt within the group of informers. The issue is further complicated by the paradox that many informers actually helped the opposition movement, partly simply by swelling its ranks, but also by actively working on opposition activities. 'Stephana', for example, was encouraged by her Stasi officer to become involved with particular religious groups whose activities were considered suspect. In many respects this task came naturally to her since the groups' interests corresponded closely with her own:

> I have to say that I would have done it anyway. It wasn't something that I wouldn't have done. They just sometimes put the idea in my head, you know; 'Do that, why don't you?', or reinforced an idea of mine to go here or there, you know, it was never

> something that went against the grain. And when I took part in something I did so because I really wanted to and I played an active role in it. I guess you could say that was schizophrenic, but I didn't even think about the fact that I had been sent there, because it was what I did anyway (A-8).

'Stephana' was therefore not only actively involved in these activities in her capacity as an unofficial employee, but was useful to the Stasi precisely because of her pre-existing contacts to such groups. This was also the case for 'Rolf'. The Stasi began to observe 'Rolf' closely in 1983, two years before he was recruited as an informer. This surveillance was put into operation after 'Rolf' had been observed carrying photo equipment in a forest close by a Soviet training ground, and it was suspected that he might be involved in foreign espionage (C-1a, p. 2). In order to establish that 'Rolf' was not involved in anti-state activities he was observed by other informers. Afterwards, he remained interesting to the Stasi only because of the contacts he had made through his interest in environmental issues. Since one of the key prerequisites for recruiting an unofficial employee was precisely that they have connections to those whom the Stasi wished to keep under surveillance, many informers do, like 'Rolf', have observer/observed elements in their biography, making the question of their relative guilt or innocence extremely complex.

Even those wholly involved in the opposition scene, generally regarded as belonging to the group of 'real victims', often worked within rather than against the status quo. Ibrahim Böhme's budding political career came to an abrupt end when, in early 1990, he was revealed to have worked for the Stasi as an unofficial employee. The news only served to confirm the suspicion which at least some of his many acquaintances had harboured for some time. Markus Meckel, for example, told journalist Birgit Lahann that Böhme had always seemed to have a considerable amount of information about certain high-ranking party officials: 'In actual fact [. . .] this was a bit suspect. But this information was also important to us' (J-49, p. 216). Although many must have seriously suspected Böhme of holding dubious contacts to the Stasi, they decided not to confront this situation, but rather to try and use it to their advantage. By doing so, they accepted and worked within the system of secrets and lies which the Stasi had created. Similarly, after 'Rolf' confessed to a man on whom he was supposed to be reporting that he was working for the Stasi, he and the man conspired for a time to write the reports which 'Rolf' subsequently supplied the Stasi with. The man hoped that if 'Rolf' turned in positive reports about him, he would be able to convince the Stasi indirectly that he was not a danger to the state, and that the travel restrictions which had been imposed upon him would subsequently be relaxed. In acting in this way, the man played along with the rules of the game as decreed by the Stasi. This was a course of action which may have presented itself as the most obvious, since its furtive and indirect nature was more than familiar:

> Conflicts were never openly displayed. It was always only ever about running away and finding a niche. A few people found refuge in the church, a few in cultural niches or in some group or other – and there was always an element of conspiracy about it all (Anglelika Barbe, J-49, p. 243).

The niches created often remained just that, and did little to threaten political and social structures. In a sense, their existence allowed people to feel that they were involved in some form of non-conformist activity and thereby to reduce any cognitive dissonance they felt about generally betraying their private convictions publicly. The reduction in dissonance which they experienced in such niches meant that they tended to comply with state policies when outside them, and perhaps partly accounted for the fact, as Eppelmann puts it, that 'there was a wide-spread hush about things, which ought never to have been kept quiet about' (J-23, p. 37). Eppelmann admits in this context that certain events organised by his church probably acted in some ways as a kind of therapy for society: 'At the end of the day we didn't exactly call upon people to overthrow the government' (ibid. p. 158). This phenomenon of an opposition which was only ever really concerned with opposing and not with taking control is one discussed by the sociologist Wolf Lepenies. Lepenies contrasts the opposition movement in the GDR to that in other Eastern European countries, describing the East German opposition as having been distinct, in that its supporters were never really concerned with gaining power (J-51, p. 32). This led to the development of a 'dissident mentality sceptical of every form of politics at the expense of effective opposition politics', in which no real thought was given as to how an individual viewpoint could become the opinion of the majority (ibid. pp. 34, 36).

By their own admission, those involved in the opposition in the GDR were certainly content at times with their position in society and may not always have really striven to overthrow the existing social order. Lutz Rathenow leaves no doubt that he and those like him suffered for their beliefs but that 'at other times life really wasn't that bad at all. "Dissidents" too had a place in the state hierarchy' (J-68, p. 1465). The injustices to which many of these dissidents were subjected were, of course, severe, and Jürgen Fuchs's portrayal of the manner in which he was mentally and physically manipulated in captivity before being forced to leave the GDR should serve as one reminder of the brutality of which the Stasi was truly capable (J-28).

* * *

In summary, a substantial proportion of the Stasi debate has been characterised by attempts to establish where any one particular individual's behaviour could be placed on a perpetrator/victim spectrum. The question of the relative guilt of Stasi informers has been one of the central issues in this discussion. Attributing responsibility to individual informers is not easy. One could say that all those who worked as informers, because they worked directly with this system, carry in some way a portion of the guilt for the injustices carried out. The network of informers was, however, only capable of functioning within a society whose citizens had on the whole come to accept and even comply with the structures that supported this system of control. There have thus been many calls for a shift away from an often futile attempt to define East Germans in terms of perpetrator/victim categories. Dönhoff argues that, since such a mass categorisation is not feasible, West Germany's role in the confrontation with recent history in the former GDR ought to be 'not to ascertain individual guilt, but to mediate in a collective process of understanding the past' (J-20, p. 12). The majority of East Germans have, however, in the face of the social and economical turmoil which unification has brought, no inclination to confront the past collectively. On a one-to-one level, such a confrontation has also not been realised. Several of those with whom I spoke were disappointed by the apparent lack of interest aroused by their confessions of having been active as a Stasi informer. 'Theodor' explained that when he told a friend that he had reported to the Stasi on him this man remained silent:

> I hoped that he would ask me some questions, but he didn't and I still remember how disappointed I was. Perhaps it was just simply too much for him. [. . .] You see, no one wanted to know how I had ended up doing what I did. I had to do all the analysis on my own. The results didn't exactly make me feel good about myself (B-3).

'Rolf' was similarly disappointed by the lack of interest he felt others displayed in really understanding what had gone on: 'No one was ever very interested in finding out how the system had worked, how the human resources had been developed, how this whole hierarchy was structured' (A-1).

Difficulties in realising fruitful dialogue in confrontations of the kind described by 'Theodor' and 'Rolf' arise partly because, having confessed to having worked for the Stasi, the person concerned often seems to await guidance as to how the conversation should progress. Stefan Heym describes how he realised with astonishment one day that a man who had come to him and confessed that he had reported on him was actually awaiting absolution (J-36, p. 92). Heym sees such behaviour as resulting from gross deficiencies in the confrontation with recent past. 'Scores of people in united Germany', he argues, have become victims of a 'confession syndrome', in which 'those who worked for the Stasi are constantly being convinced that it will all be okay if they just come forward and confess their sins in the media, while others lust greedily for these sensational confessions' (ibid.).

Another factor underlying the apparent lack of willingness to analyse the structures which supported the system of power in the GDR results from a sense of common identity within the former East. Much of the anger which was originally directed at those who had abused power within the GDR was later focused on West Germans who, as the full economic scale of unification began to be felt in the former East, were often apportioned blame for rendering East Germans the victims and losers. Faced with the demands of coming to terms with unemployment and a new, less rigid, social structure, many East Germans indulge in what has become known as Eastalgia, nostalgia for the GDR. This sentimental reminiscing about the past does not facilitate a critical confrontation with the past. For this reason, the less rosy aspects of life in the GDR are often conveniently forgotten in order to allow full indulgence in a shared sense of victimisation and in a mourning for what has been lost. Originally, many more East Germans considered themselves victims of direct observation, and the extent of the Stasi's might was exaggerated when confronting the past. The more evil the Stasi was portrayed as being, the easier it was to justify conformity, leading Jurek Becker to observe:

> The eagerness with which the Stasi's evil deeds are now being flaunted and tracked down seems to me to be an attempt on many people's part to undo their own subordination. The greater the menace one was subjected to is portrayed as having been, the more acceptable the way in which one gave in to it for years has to be. If you did actually act as the perfect subject, shouldn't you at least be allowed to believe that you didn't have any other choice? (J-33, p. 77).

The feeling of hatred towards Stasi employees faded in the years following unification, and many East Germans began to forget or disregard the severe injustices inflicted on what is, in reality, a very small minority who were not content to conform in the past. The small group of 'real victims' were left marginalised and often despised for their attempts to keep the debate alive. Chaim Noll referred to this increasingly prevalent readiness to forgive and forget as an 'all-encompassing pulp of reconciliation', within which compliance with the system becomes accepted as having been the norm and opposition as deviant (J-65, pp. 98–9). Both groups at either end of the guilt spectrum, that is those of 'real victims' and 'real perpetrators' represent minorities and are to many an unwelcome reminder of their own conformity and of the serious flaws in a state whose loss they wish to mourn. A wide-spread societal confrontation with the Stasi's methods and structures did not, therefore, take place in the years following the fall of the Wall. Emphasis was placed rather on a more superficial sensationalist approach to the Stasi legacy, in which the deeds of specific individuals were highlighted, rather than general tendencies within the collective. Many East Germans became increasingly eager to ignore the failings of the past system, preferring rather, depending on their age and on their immediate social and economic situation, either to embrace the new system or to reminisce about the former one. In doing so, they defined new categories of good and evil relevant to the existing political situation, rendering, at least in the interim, the old ones and the debate concerning them increasingly obsolete.

9

LOOKING BACK

THE ART OF MEMORY

> I'm thankful that I seem to have forgotten very early on. How could I have lived all those years knowing that, how could I have continued to write, who could I have confided in? (Christa Wolf, J-99, p. 203).

In early 1993, the news broke that the celebrated East German writer Christa Wolf had, in the late 1950s and early 1960s, had contacts with the Stasi as an informer under the cover name of 'Margarete'. A fierce attack was launched on her person by her critics old and new, in what seemed to be almost a replay of the controversy which had surrounded the publication of her novel, *Was bleibt*, three years previously (J-104). After the hysteria had subsided, and the evidence from the files was examined more objectively, it was generally accepted that the extent of Wolf's compliance had been minimal and had encompassed only a brief period of time. It was argued in her defence that Wolf and her husband had been subjected to well over twenty years of what was, at times, round-the-clock surveillance as a result of the very much more critical stance she had developed towards the state after an initial period of youthful political *naïveté* (J-99, pp. 201, 340). This was undoubtedly the case, yet the real shock lay not in the fact that Wolf had held contacts of this kind with the Stasi per se, but rather in her apparent forgetting of these events until confronted with the documentation of them in her files. Wolf claimed that when she read in her files that she had been active as an informer it caught her 'fully unprepared' (ibid. pp. 143–4).

In not admitting to having worked for the Stasi until the irrefutable evidence from the files lay before her, Wolf displayed what has come to be a classic behaviour pattern witnessed in informers. The person concerned denies having held such contacts to the Stasi until evidence from the files is produced which renders any further denial futile. At this point they claim to have suppressed all previous knowledge of the contact until the documentation has evoked these lost memories. Often this memory jolt is so effective that informers then seem to remember many details and try to relativise their past actions by claiming, for example, that they never reported anything of consequence and cannot be held responsible for causing any harm to fellow East Germans.

The silence on the part of former Stasi employees until they are unmasked has infuriated those who were under Stasi observation. Many hold the view that this silence is almost more reprehensible than the deed itself. Advocating the resignation of Brandenburg's Premier, Manfred Stolpe, Vera Wollenberger said that, whereas Stolpe's co-operation with the Stasi was in itself highly questionable, 'even worse, indeed fatal, is however the fact that he kept quiet about it afterwards' (I-16).

There are obvious practical reasons behind a conscious decision to keep quiet about one's Stasi connections. Former informers may fear being sacked, or may be concerned about the negative social implications which potentially follow such a confession. Rainer Schedlinski had the following to say on the matter:

> As long as journalists complain about the lack of willingness on the part of informers to confess but at the same time only accept schizophrenia, corruption, blackmail or the post-modern loss of the notion of truth as valid explanations for having worked for the Stasi, it is they who are ignorant. Those concerned will, of course, never admit to this truth, because if they did they would be lying (J-77, p. 75).

Some of those who became frustrated with the unwillingness of former Stasi employees to admit to what they had done simply took matters into their own hands. Wolf Biermann, for example, sensationally outed the writer Sascha Anderson as having been an informer in a speech given on the receipt of the Büchner prize, a prestigious literary award. Biermann referred to Anderson as 'the untalented gossip Sascha Arsehole, a Stasi snoop who's still coolly pretending to be the son of the Muses and hoping that his files never turn up' (J-10, p. 300).

Informers such as Anderson often decide after there can be no doubt in their own minds that they were bona fide Stasi informers not to admit to this fact publicly until they are effectively forced to. Christa Wolf herself waited well over half a year after viewing the evidence in her files before she decided to make this information public. Yet, what of the period before someone is confronted with evidence from the files? Can the statements of those such as Wolf who claim that they had actually suppressed the knowledge of their actions be taken at face value? Is it possible that the desire not to have been a Stasi informer is so strong that it can actually block the memories of this period of someone's past life? The following section will address these questions with the aid of several studies into the psychology of memory.

* * *

Psychologists researching autobiographical memory have tended in recent times to reject copy theories of memory, which traditionally supported the notion that what was remembered was an exact replica of a past event. Michael Ross, for example, researched extensively into autobiographical memory, finding further evidence that individuals employ 'implicit theories of self to construct their personal histories' (J-74, p. 341). In other words, people will tend to use their current perception of self to infer their past behaviour. Unless information is salient which leads us to believe that personal attitudes and therefore behaviour have undergone change, then we will tend to exaggerate the similarity of past to present. When Ross and Conway had two groups of subjects listen to differing statements about health care they found that those subjects who heard that frequent tooth brushing could damage teeth, reported brushing their teeth less often than those who heard a message praising tooth brushing (J-75, pp. 127–8). Ross and Conway concluded that since people are 'cognitive conservatives who bias their memories so as to deny change and maintain temporal consistency and coherence', 'attitudes that are salient and are judged relevant to the behaviour in question may guide reconstructive memory' (ibid. pp. 128, 135). This is the basic principle of 'Dissonance Theory', formulated in 1973 by Goethals and Reckman, which proposed that since individuals feel uncomfortable when they realise current attitudes clash with prior ones, they tend to reduce this discomfort (dissonance) by forgetting their original stance and presuming that their opinions have not altered (ibid. p. 131).

The results of the above research may shed light on the phenomenon of apparent forgetting witnessed in former Stasi informers. The majority of East German citizens conformed at least superficially with state policies for most of the GDR's forty year existence, with many displaying their genuine dissatisfaction and disillusionment only in late 1989. It is often claimed that the demonstrations throughout East Germany at this time played a major contributing factor to the fall of the regime, and, although many GDR citizens were taken by surprise at the speed with which unification was achieved, these events tended, at least in the Western media, to be interpreted as an indication that the *Volk* was liberating itself from the throes of communism and embracing the capitalist system. This course of events, one could suppose, led to a change in the self-perception of many East Germans, who now considered themselves to have been active opponents of the Party. Applying Ross's findings, that individuals tend to believe their attitudes remain constant over time, one could suppose that those who were dissatisfied with state practices in 1989 would tend to presume this had been their general attitude before this time and, since people believe behaviour reflects attitude, could well believe that they displayed this discontentment prior to 1989. This would partly account for the fact that many are reluctant to accept that they were not under direct surveillance (F-8, p. 52). It may also be possible that the perception of oneself as a non-conformer is strengthened when individuals reconstruct memories of past behaviour on the basis of present, more critical, attitudes towards the GDR. This is not to say that informers cannot remember having had any contacts to the Stasi per se, rather that they remember the contacts as such, that they were visited by a Stasi officer on several occasions, for example, but strive to convince themselves that this contact never took on the concrete form of an agreement to work as an unofficial employee. As discussed, Ross has shown that people generally have difficulty accurately reconstructing their personal histories and infer their past behaviour from current attitudes and perceptions of self. This self-image is currently being re-evaluated and perhaps re-defined for the majority of former East Germans in the context of the vast societal upheaval which they have witnessed. When the element of the social and psychological undesirability of having been an informer is added to the equation, it is hardly surprising that, in order even just to preserve their self-esteem, a significant number of people may apply a sort of 'can't have been' approach to constructing their own personal history. This is confirmed by a statement from Jutta Braband, who resigned her political mandate for the PDS after viewing her Stasi files. Braband described her shock at being confronted with the details of her contact to the Stasi which she found in these files: 'What I remembered was incredibly harmless stuff. I had a version of the whole story in my head which preserved my self-image' (I-41, p. 40).

The issue is further complicated by the fact that even when they were actively working for the Stasi, informers may well have had a complex relationship to the self. Commenting on the cases of Anderson and Schedlinski, the journalist Mathias Ehlert said that: 'Their self-image differed fundamentally from the truths in the files. [. . .] They were bound to both systems – holding unofficial talks with representatives of a power which they completely rejected in their official self-image' (I-28).

* * *

A key issue which is often neglected in a consideration of the phenomenon of apparent forgetting on the part of Stasi informers is the question of terminology. The term 'unofficial employee' has only come into general usage since 1989, and although 'Stephana' was very much aware that by 1989 she had been working with the Stasi for approximately four years, she did not suspect how commonplace such a liaison actually was. After the events of 1989 it took her quite some time to realise that she too was one of the apparently large group of 'unofficial employees' suddenly being given so much media attention. 'Stephana' says that until this time she had always considered her situation a 'one-off' and describes how she constantly asked herself, 'Am I one of them, or am I not?' as she gradually faced the truth about her past (A-8). It is not merely the label 'unofficial employee' which is novel for the informer, but much of the terminology which was developed and applied in this highly refined system of observation and control. The entire Stasi debate is thus conducted in what are, for most, previously unfamiliar linguistic concepts, and informers must first identify themselves with the terminology used to define their past actions and re-evaluate and re-define their self-image and personal history in order to incorporate these structures.

Linked to the question of terminology is the fact that in the debate concerning the relative guilt or innocence of Stasi informers much emphasis has been placed on the details rather than on the essence of the contact. As discussed in Chapter 6, this was particularly true of the debate concerning Manfred Stolpe. The Stolpe Committee spent much time on what proved to be the futile attempt to establish, for example, where, when, and from whom Stolpe had received a specific decoration. It is conceivable that Stolpe was consciously lying, but just as plausible that he was no longer sure of the exact course of events surrounding this episode. Once again it is possible to draw on evidence from studies into memory which indicate that an individual may have difficulty recalling their whereabouts even for significant life events. Larsen, a Danish psychologist, kept a diary for six months and, without first consulting it, later tested his memory of his whereabouts on particular days. He found that he had remembered hearing about the Chernobyl disaster on the radio in the morning. His diary told him, however, that he had been 'at Pia's place just after work' when he heard the news (J-103, pp. 289–90). Larsen's recall was also inaccurate for his whereabouts when he discovered that the Swedish Prime Minister, Olaf Palme, had been assassinated, an event of considerable impact for a Scandinavian. Larsen found these memories so vivid that only the diary convinced him that they were false.

In the Stolpe debate, no certainty could be ever established on matters such as the details surrounding the awarding of the service medal. The accounts from Stolpe and the Stasi officers questioned by the Committee were often vague and contradictory, and the whole issue became at times merely comical. By placing the emphasis on the details of Stolpe's Stasi contacts rather than on their general nature it seemed that an individual was free from guilt if certain formal criteria had not been met. The silence on the part of some informers may be partly a result of this focus on detail in the confrontation with the Stasi legacy. Some informers may attempt, for example, to convince themselves that they did not actually sign a formal statement of commitment and were perhaps not registered as an unofficial employee. A confrontation with individual behaviour is not facilitated in this atmosphere where terminology rather than substance is often the foremost factor in deciding a person's fate.

In summary, there are many possible reasons why informers remain silent about their Stasi contacts, particularly if these contacts lie, as they did in Christa Wolf's case, in the distant past. An altered image of self, combined with the social undesirability of having been an informer, may lead the individual to adopt a 'can't have been' attitude to the confrontation with the past, believing that present attitudes must reflect past behaviour. The Stasi debate has, furthermore, been characterised by the often sensational unmasking of certain individuals as unofficial employees. Ultimately, however, they only seem to suffer serious repercussions for having been so if absolute proof, generally in the form of an official statement of commitment, can be produced. In this sense, the certified unofficial Stasi employees have, to some extent, been made scapegoats in the reckoning with the GDR past, and a consideration of individual roles outside this framework has not taken place. Since informers can lose their jobs on account of having worked for the Stasi, there are no legal, only moral incentives for admitting to having done so, especially if there is any element of doubt whatsoever on the part of the individual concerned.

Once the moment has come when they can no longer publicly or privately deny having worked for the Stasi, some informers seem more than keen to talk about this fact. Since none of them approached him, Klaus Hugler, a target of Stasi observation, decided after reading his file to contact those informers who he discovered had been reporting on him. Although these individuals had remained silent until he approached them, they responded immediately he did so, almost as if they had been waiting for this moment. The informer 'Gerhard Winzer', for example, got in touch the day after Hugler wrote to him (J-37, p. 93). 'Fritz Wunok' phoned Hugler immediately after receiving his letter and arranged to travel from Bavaria to meet with Hugler in Potsdam the very next day. (J-37, pp. 94–5). This urgency would suggest that these informers had been holding out as long as possible, hoping that perhaps their Stasi past would remain undisclosed. Perhaps Hugler's informers expressed such an urgency to see him as they hoped to persuade him to keep the matter quiet. Yet, this explanation alone would not account for why the informers I spoke to were prepared to talk. Although they had been assured that they would remain anonymous, there was undoubtedly a certain amount of risk involved in engaging in such dialogue with a complete stranger. When I asked them why they had decided to speak to me, I received varying responses. 'Rolf' and 'Stephana' both said that they felt the need to speak of this aspect of their biography in an attempt to come to terms with it (A-1; A-8). 'Falke' and 'Katrin' emphasised that it was important that their perspective be heard (A-3; A-9). I suspect that most of my interviewees were glad to have someone to relate their story to, and that talking to me afforded them the welcome opportunity of doing so without having to fear any negative repercussions which might follow the admission of having worked for the Stasi in other forums. Walter Schilling suggests that many informers do wish to break their silence, but simply do not find the strength to do so:

> All informers must be outed – with the emphasis on the word outed. One of them even said that to me: 'You had to out me – I couldn't have done it myself.' The power of the conspiracy is so great that they can't do it – like those who can't admit that they have an addiction (F-13, p. 98).

In cases where informers do sooner or later admit to having worked for the Stasi, a pattern of selective memory, or rather selective confrontation, often develops in the way in which they consequently narrate the past. These people will tend to maintain that they are certain of particular details of the work they did for the Stasi, while still claiming not to remember, for example, ever having received financial rewards, having met with Stasi officers in a secret location or at what point the contact came to an end. Even when informers do finally admit to what they have done and are prepared to talk of the past, this confrontation is then one which is fraught with denial, suppression, half-truths and ambiguities. The public debate concerning informers has, to a large extent, been concerned with the moral issue of how such individuals should confront this aspect of their biographies. Statements made by former Stasi informers are often disregarded if they do not correspond to factual evidence, and an analysis of these statements and therefore of the way in which such individuals actually were and are confronting their past tends to be neglected. Yet this latter issue is particularly worthy of study as, after all, the 'importance of oral testimony may often lie not in its adherence to facts but rather in its divergence from them, where imagination, symbolism, desire break in' (J-67, p. 100).

RETROSPECTIVE LEGENDS?

In order to cope with the shock of discovering that they now belong to the group of socially stigmatised 'unofficial employees', onetime informers often employ a by now standard repertoire of justification arguments in defence of their actions. Very few, for example, are prepared to admit publicly to any feelings of guilt whatsoever. They tend rather to trivialise and defend their actions. These justification strategies might at first seem to be feeble excuses for morally questionable behaviour. When they are more closely examined, such statements can, however, provide valuable insights into the way in which informers publicly and privately confront their Stasi past, as well as into the way in which they viewed the contacts to the Stasi at the time when they were active.

Perhaps the most common justification strategy is a normalisation/trivialisation approach, employed, for example, by 'Katrin' when she claims that as a convinced patriot, it was 'the most normal thing in the world' for her to agree to work as an informer (A-9). In a pamphlet advertising her candidacy for election to the German parliament, she writes that she initially viewed the contact to the Stasi 'as contributing to the protection of the GDR – and only in the course of this contact did doubts about the purpose and legitimacy of what I was doing begin to arise'. 'Katrin' would put a cross in her diary on the days when she was to meet her Stasi officer, but thought no more of it (A-9). The Stasi files relating to 'Katrin' give a slightly different perspective. 'Katrin's' Stasi officer noted that after she arrived in Leningrad, where she was to be active as an informer while carrying out her studies, she did not abide by an agreement made in the GDR to contact him by telephone. Several months passed until she was prompted by a letter to get in touch with him. A meeting was arranged soon afterwards, at which she excused herself by saying that the telephone number given to her in the GDR had slipped her mind. (C-7b, p. 19). The Stasi officer subsequently noted in the report of the meeting that 'Katrin' had seemed quite uncomfortable when excusing her absence in this way (ibid.). This could indicate that the story about the forgotten telephone number was fabricated and that for some reason 'Katrin' had begun to feel that working for the Stasi would not be the most normal thing in the world after all. The Stasi was, in fact, more than aware that its informers tended to suffer from scruples and documented methods of reducing these by aiming to convince informers that their actions were morally justifiable. In an introductory speech to a seminar on the work with unofficial employees, Erich Mielke stated that: 'It must be made clear to every unofficial employee how fundamentally this secret work for the MfS differs from the snooping activities of enemy agents' (F-5, I, p. 536).

There were, of course, cases of informers who genuinely did not doubt the morality of their actions. In the files held on 'Falke', there seems to be no indication that he at any time expressed doubts about his role (C-3a, b). In conversation, 'Falke' emphasises repeatedly how much this work was merely part of his daily routine, and when I ask him if he felt relieved after it became known that he had been an informer, he simply replies: 'It didn't bother me at all' (A-3). Cases such as 'Falke' are, however, rather the exception. Former unofficial employees are more often reluctant to admit to the genuine doubts they experienced as they would then be unable to employ this particular justification strategy of normalisation/ trivialisation.

At the time when they were active as such, informers could only guess at how many others were working for the Stasi. Some were flattered to believe that they belonged to a select few GDR citizens deemed worthy of carrying out this important task. 'Theodor', for example, considered the invitation to work for the Stasi to be 'an incredible honour' (A-2). 'Stephana' needed a long time after the fall of the Wall to come to terms with the fact that she belonged to the large group of informers, since she had always considered her situation to be a 'one-off' (A-8). Whereas, at the time of their active involvement with the Stasi, some informers tended to consider their situation special, out of the ordinary, and perhaps this feeling even led to increased motivation, the same individuals justify their actions today by stressing exactly the opposite. That is to say that the contacts were an integral part of their daily lives, a regular feature of their routine, which, since it was in essence trivial, even banal, was morally justifiable and as such never really a source of doubt or scruples.

A further common justification strategy is to argue that one's role as a Stasi informer was one of a mediator or helper. This was witnessed in one of the most sensational revelations from the Stasi files, the case of Knud Wollenberger, who was discovered to have informed on his wife Vera for many years under the cover name 'Donald'. 'Donald' admitted publicly to no feelings of guilt for his actions, claiming that in talks with this Stasi officer:

> I was reporting on myself as much as anyone. [. . .] Often I was telling him what I said and did. These ideas were all part of what should have been possible in this country. Our activities were very public. I tried to influence my handler to change his thinking. By telling the Stasi about our ideas, I'm sure I influenced them (J-73, p. 378).

'Donald' was not alone in trying to argue that what he was doing was actually of benefit to the opposition scene. Yet, although both the informer and the Stasi often endeavoured to keep the belief alive that there was a politically and morally justifiable purpose to working as an unofficial employee, this ceased in many cases to be a real motivating factor. In other cases, events took exactly the opposite course, where an informer recruited on the basis of 'compromising material' later developed a sense of purpose as an internal justification and, therefore, coping strategy. This was the case for 'Stephana', who, at least initially, understood her co-operation as a direct consequence of the threats made against her at recruitment because of her role in the attempted escape from East Germany of an acquaintance of hers. Later, she tried to find meaning and purpose in the contact to the Stasi:

> I sort of gradually had the feeling that I was acting as a sort of mediator, ensuring that these events could take place, you know. And of course I didn't always tell it exactly as it was, but portrayed the meetings as a lot less reactionary than they actually were (A-8).

The word 'gradually' is significant in 'Stephana's' statement as it indicates that she developed this personal legitimation argument over time. It is evident that statements such as these are not merely justifications which informers employ now in a public forum, but ones which they developed and used at the time when they worked for the Stasi as a means of privately rationalising behaviour. This phenomenon led one commentator to remark of Knud Wollenberger's arguments: 'As off-putting as Wollenberger's smug tone is, it is hard to recognise where the boundaries lie between retrospective legend and original conviction' (I-38, p. 36). This particular justification/coping strategy was at times not entirely unfounded. Evidence can be found in the files of occasions when informers were clearly trying to use their position to benefit others. 'Sonnenblume' stressed in a report that an acquaintance who had applied for a visa to visit a relative in Sweden was not planning to use this opportunity to flee the GDR (C-8b, pp. 21–2). Indeed, the majority of the reports 'Sonnenblume' gave were overwhelmingly positive character descriptions of her friends and acquaintances. She tells me that she made a conscious decision to write only positively of others, hoping that perhaps the person in question might benefit from such a report (A-10). Although at other times the reports he gave were undoubtedly potentially harmful, 'Fuchs' did on at least one occasion report that the inmates in the prison where he worked had been complaining about the bad quality of the food and medical care (C-5b, p. 349). In this case, 'Fuchs' certainly appears to have been trying to exercise any influence he may have had to bring about a change for the better. This information is, indeed, judged as 'significant' and measures are suggested to improve the situation (ibid.). Even Rainer Eppelmann, who was so strongly opposed to Manfred Stolpe staying in power as the Premier of Brandenburg after the extent of his Stasi contacts came to light, had to admit: 'Manfred Stolpe helped many people, including me, on many occasions' (J-23, p. 295). In many informers' careers, there were undoubtedly moments where they tried in some way to benefit others. These moments were emphasised by informers at the time when they were active in order to preserve their self-image just as they are stressed now in order to justify having worked for the Stasi.

Ironically, the Stasi did not always pay heed to more critical information supplied by informers, which could, had it been acted upon, have benefited not only others but the organisation itself. When asked in 1986 about the general mood of the population, 'Reiner' reported that many fellow citizens had expressed the view that they saw no point in voting (C-4b, III, p. 229). 'Falke' was equally critical when he reported that some of his colleagues were of the opinion that another colleague had been too harshly treated when he lost his Party membership as a result of a minor misdemeanour (C-3b, II, p. 9). In 1989 'Falke' also reported that many older comrades believed that mistakes had been made in the running of the country and were disappointed and disillusioned (ibid. II, pp. 362–3). These pieces of information were indications of general and widespread dissatisfaction within the population, yet they were not judged as significant. Perhaps this can be explained by the fact that the Stasi nurtured in its internal ideology a somewhat simplistic concept of the enemy, defined as those individuals 'who individually or in groups purposefully develop political and ideological opinions and stances which are fundamentally opposed to socialism' (F-3, p. 110). The work with informers concentrated on the fight against these specific individuals, and signs of general decay and of disillusionment within the ranks of those who, as a group, were basically faithful citizens, such as 'Falke's' colleagues in the police force, were consequently ignored.

A further justification strategy is encountered when the Stasi is portrayed as being omnipotent and unable to be resisted. This perception of the Stasi as 'perfectly organised apparatus' was one which was dominant in the immediate post-Wall period (J-109, p. 22). It is an image which informers seeking to justify their Stasi contacts often exploit. The mightier the Stasi is seen to be, the more informers are justified in claiming that attempts to resist recruitment or to end the contact would have been futile. By exaggerating the Stasi's omnipotence, informers aim to impose an element of inevitability on their actions. This is a legitimation strategy employed not only by informers but also by those very much further up the power hierarchy in the GDR. Politburo member Kurt Hager, for example, claimed that he would rather not have lived in the Stasi compound to the north of Berlin, describing it as 'forced captivity' (J-33, p. 75). On hearing Hager's statement, the writer Jurek Becker commented wryly that 'all at once it dawned upon us that even the Politburo members themselves were victims of the Politburo' (ibid.). It is this frequent use of a vocabulary of necessity in legitimation attempts of former political agitators in the GDR which particularly disturbs Becker since it denies the notion of free will and of individual responsibility: 'This *I had to* cannot be challenged, those who say it protect themselves by doing so from any embarrassing questioning' (J-33, p. 74). This strategy is commonplace and whilst he does admit to having experienced scruples about his actions as an informer 'Theodor' reduces some of his individual responsibility by claiming that there was 'a certain necessity' to his actions: 'It's a terrible thing when you *have to* spy on a friend' (A-2).

By justifying behaviour in this way, informers imply that they cannot be considered responsible for their actions since they were to a certain extent environmentally determined:

> We do not hold people responsible for their reflexes – for example, for coughing in church. We hold them responsible for their operant behaviour – for whispering in church or remaining in church while coughing. But there are variables which are responsible for whispering as well as coughing, and these may be just as inexorable. When we recognise this, we are likely to drop

> the notion of responsibility altogether and with it the notion of free will as an inner causal agent
>
> (B. F. Skinner, J-60, p. 58).

In the justification strategies of 'Sonnenblume' and 'Karin Lenz', the inexorable variable which they define as being largely responsible for their willingness to work for the Stasi is the hold which their respective Stasi officers had over them. As discussed previously, 'Karin Lenz' described her officer 'Detlef' as a kind of psychological mentor, who acted as a substitute psychiatrist and whom she could call at any time of day or night (J-45, p. 43). 'Karin Lenz' thus reduces the individual responsibility she carries for her actions by portraying herself as a victim whose weaknesses were cleverly exploited by the Stasi. Similarly 'Sonnenblume' describes her officer 'Roland' as a 'devil-like magnet', thereby doubly emphasising the inevitability of succumbing to him (J-110, p. 260).

The Stasi was, in many respects, a mighty and powerful institution whose cunning it was not always easy to resist. An examination of the written legacy of the organisation will quickly reveal, however, that it certainly was not perfectly organised. The mythification of this institution as such serves the needs of those who seek to justify their conformist behaviour and is therefore a frequently employed legitimation strategy by former Stasi informers as well as by many who are now keen to explain away their own compliance with the power hierarchy in the GDR.

The final justification strategy worthy of mention here is that of relativisation. This is displayed when informers emphasise that there were very definite limits to their willingness to co-operate with the wishes of the Stasi. By doing so, they aim to minimise personal culpability by stressing that they did not comply to the extent to which they could potentially have done so. This coping/legitimation strategy is the opposite approach to the one discussed above. Instead of justifying their behaviour by emphasising their helplessness in the face of the Stasi's omnipotence, informers claim to have been strong enough and sufficiently in control of the situation to withstand some of the pressure exerted by the Stasi officers and to impose certain limitations on the nature of the work carried out. After the shock revelation that she, too, had worked for the Stasi, Christa Wolf claimed: 'I never told them anything that could not be heard anyway at any public gathering' (J-99, p. 305). Since Wolf gave several detailed character descriptions and reported on the connections which a West German writer held in the GDR, the validity of this statement is questionable. This relativisation strategy is extremely common and was employed by several of my interviewees, including 'Katrin':

> I didn't report anything which I had gone to great lengths to find out. I didn't go and read her letters or anything and that's why I think that the word snoop just isn't applicable. [. . .] I never deliberately got information out of anyone or went to some party or other only so as I could report on it afterwards (A-9).

At times it may, indeed, have been the case that informers only gave information which was known to them anyway, although this does not necessarily justify the breach of trust which was involved in reporting these details to the Stasi. The amount of truth contained in relativisation statements such as these is, furthermore, always open to question. 'Stephana', for example, employs this strategy when she insists that she very seldom named names when asked about those present at the religious meetings she attended: 'I always tried to talk myself out of it by saying that I couldn't remember the names. I hardly ever referred to people by name, because I always said that I didn't have a good memory for names' (A-8). The reports written by 'Stephana's' Stasi officer suggest, however, that this was only really the case initially, when 'Stephana' is noted as being unable to identify by name various people at the gatherings she is questioned about (C-6b, I, pp. 54–5, 60–1). There are two possible explanations for this. The first is that by using information from other informers, the Stasi officer was simply able to work out to whom exactly 'Stephana' was referring; or, alternatively, that during the course of her work for the Stasi 'Stephana's' resistance weakened and she did in fact increasingly refer to those present by name.

Rather than by referring to the content of their meetings with the Stasi, 'Falke' and 'Fuchs' relativise their past actions by imposing a contextual limitation on them. They maintain that they considered the contact to the Stasi almost as a duty in their line of work, which, since 'Falke' was an officer in criminal investigation, and 'Fuchs' a trainer in a high-security prison, involved a considerable amount of contact to Stasi officers on a daily basis (A-3; A-6). I ask 'Falke' if he then considers himself to be different from a common snoop, a *Spitzel*, the derogatory term by which informers are often referred to. He pauses for some time before answering:

> Now you're asking me of course . . . I can't really answer that very easily . . . No . . . snoop . . . I imagine something different when I think of a snoop . . . if I had quite deliberately taken on and carried out specific tasks, and I really didn't do anything like that (A-3).

Perhaps 'Falke's' last words in answer to this question best sum up the strategy of relativising having worked as an informer. After a long pause, which itself was quite uncharacteristic for him, he finally says: 'Yeah, sure, it was really a form of snooping. Yeah, sure, sure ... but not a 100 per cent so' (ibid.).

The way in which 'Falke' relativises his role is typical, and the vast majority of Stasi employees claim that no harm was ever caused to an individual as a direct result of their actions. This prevailing tendency has led to the image of the informer as someone with whom dialogue is virtually impossible, someone who is not prepared to admit to any feelings of guilt whatsoever for their actions. 'It seems that the culprits,' observed Jürgen Fuchs, 'forgave themselves long ago' (J-78, p. 308). The unwillingness to acknowledge personal responsibility is often tolerated to a lesser extent when encountered in the figure of the informer than in those higher up the power hierarchy, and Biermann refers to this phenomenon as the 'irregularity in the geometric curve of our feelings of hatred' (I-44, p. 89). Publicly, in fear of the legal and social implications of admitting to guilt, informers generally insist that they are blameless if no direct harm can be proved to have been caused as a result of their actions. The reluctance of informers to admit to their personal guilt is intensified by the fact that no other individuals or groups seem prepared to accept a moral responsibility for the injustices which were carried out within the GDR: 'Where there is no guilt it need not be atoned. How are the ordinary people supposed to recognise their modest sins if even the bad guys act as though they were benign?' (I-78, p. 73).

The issue of whether Stasi informers are prepared to admit to any feelings of guilt, publicly or privately, is further complicated by the fact that many have actually suffered since the fall of the Wall as a result of having worked for the Stasi and have no desire to subject themselves to the possible repercussions of such an admission. These individuals often perceive themselves as double victims of unification, that is as East Germans and as Stasi informers. A very small proportion of informers have actually been fired from their jobs in public service, yet their Stasi past still haunts them. They are, for example, aware that they must act within certain limitations if they do not want this fact to become public knowledge. Three of those with whom I spoke regretted that they could not become involved in political movements to the extent they wished. Were they to do so and at some point to be screened, they would run the risk of damaging not only their personal reputation, but also that of their party. Other informers have been restricted in different ways. 'Fuchs' and 'Falke' both lost their jobs because of having worked for the Stasi. 'Katrin' was forced to resign her political mandate. 'Theodor' took early retirement as he anticipated that if he did not do so he would sooner or later be unmasked and dismissed. Many informers still fear that their secret will come out. Most tend to have confessed that they worked for the Stasi to only a select few or kept quiet about it completely, and immediate material and social concerns often override any feelings of guilt they might otherwise experience. Ultimately, the predominant sentiment of the informer is that of self-pity; on the one hand because of their immediate situation, on the other for having supported a now defeated system which has been shown not only to have been corrupt, but to have in many ways been a bureaucratic shambles. This feeling of self-pity is prevalent in any discussion with former Stasi informers, as highlighted by the following words from Dirk Schneider, a previously prominent Green Party member:

> I just can't do anything anymore and I accept that. That's fair enough. I always went in for open politics and had this secret which I had to carry round with me as it were. I felt really bad about that and I don't think that it was OK – I'll tell you that. That's a political mistake, a fundamental mistake – but you can't make any more out of it – except that I've put myself off the map and in an impossible situation, that I'm not credible. No one wants to know me because I had dealings with that dictatorship. That's very clear (H-1).

Schneider clearly feels sorry for himself and when I ask her whether she feels guilt on account of her Stasi past, 'Stephana's' response also indicates that the sentiments of regret which she does experience are often ones of self-pity: 'Yes, yes . . . let's say guilty, furious, disappointed' (A-8). 'Rolf', likewise, does experience guilt, but also deeply regrets the difficulties which his Stasi connections caused him personally:

> First I think that I was terribly naïve – then I feel really miserable when I think about that time – when I went into that flat and met them there – really horrible feelings – and, . . . yes, on the whole I accept what I did and say that I would like to erase this period from my file. I'm not saying that I feel really sorry and that I want to rip it out, I'm owning up to it now, but I regret that time and all the nerves and drama that we had here at home because of it (A-1).

Informers are able to further intensify their feelings of self-pity by emphasising that it was the coincidence of circumstance which led them to work for the Stasi. 'Fuchs' argues that the chain of coincidence which resulted in him becoming a Stasi informer began as far back as the time when he and his family were on the run from the approaching Red Army at the end of the World War Two: 'It is pure chance [. . .] that we went that way – the result of many chance occurrences. If I, if we had only, let's say, kept going all night when we were on the run, I would perhaps have ended up in Bavaria' (A-6). 'Fuchs' also emphasised the coincidence of circumstance within East Germany. When I asked him if harm was ever caused to anyone as a direct result of his reports, he admitted that he once consciously tried to prevent a colleague whose competence he doubted becoming his successor. 'Fuchs' now argues that he actually helped the man, as, had this man stepped into his shoes at work, then he too 'would have had to do the informer bit', and would, like 'Fuchs', have lost his job after the Wall came down (A-6). 'Sonnenblume' also believes that it was not just a question of strength of character which led to some individuals becoming Stasi informers and some not, but also one of 'favourable circumstances' (A-10). There is, indeed, some truth in the argument that particular individuals were unlucky to be asked to become unofficial Stasi employees, when it is considered that these individuals were not informers in the sense that they occasionally approached the Stasi and offered information, but were rather carefully selected and screened before a detailed plan of action concerning their recruitment was devised and implemented.

In summary, informers use a variety of strategies to rationalise their behaviour. It is important to consider that these are not merely a means of publicly justifying behaviour, but are also coping strategies which help to reduce and relativise feelings of guilt, which many experience now and experienced while they were active for the Stasi. These are feelings to which they do not readily admit. Many did, at least periodically, harbour doubts about their actions. Today, the coping strategies which they have developed often do not allow them to admit to these doubts, and a feeling of self-pity dominates the confrontation with the past. Informers tend to deny all guilt in the public forum. Privately, they are unsure of what they have done and uncertain of what the future may hold. These varying and conflicting emotions are perhaps best summed up by 'Theodor' in the following words:

> You know, since 1990, and that's four years now, you've had to live with the stigma of having been an informer. You can justify it to yourself if you want, but you're still stuck with it. And . . . and

it turns out that it was all so pointless. [...] I regret not having taken a more critical stance towards our senile leaders. [...] We certainly spoke about the problems, yeah [...] made all those typical GDR jokes. We made these openly, even with the Stasi officers. But in the end we were in charge of the system, and that means that we weren't true to our ethos to be revolutionaries and to change the world. I regret that we all became so horribly petty bourgeois. And my time as an unofficial employee or as an informer or whatever you want to call it is, of course, a part of that (A-2).

10

RE-ACQUISITION OF BIOGRAPHY

When you read your files you come to the point where you have to re-evaluate your own past.

(Gerd Poppe, I-7)

The implementation of the Stasi Document Law (StUG) on 29 December 1991 meant that, theoretically, an end was in sight to the mass speculation about who had or had not been involved in the Stasi's wide-scale surveillance and control measures. The debate over the law's specifications had been heated, leading Jens Reich to remark that the negotiations had been characterised by 'Drama instead of politics, emotionally charged gestures instead of negotiations' (I-74, p. 50). No other post-communist nation passed such a comprehensive law at this early stage concerning the files of its former Secret Service. The Polish writer Andrzej Szczypiorski considered this method of dealing with the cumbersome Stasi legacy flawed, arguing that the Germans were only torturing themselves by confronting the harsh truths contained in the dossiers. Szczypiorski imagined a scenario where his own wife had informed on his activities to the Secret Service. He proposed that this fact alone would amount to the first great defeat in his life. Becoming aware of this situation, however, through the possibilities of such a law, would constitute a second defeat, indeed, would destroy his life completely (J-94, p. 368). On the other side of the German/Polish border the response to the StUG was immense, indicating that many did not share Szczypiorski's fears concerning the potentially traumatic personal consequences of viewing one's Stasi file. Hundreds of thousands of ordinary citizens clearly wished to discover exactly what role the Stasi had played in shaping their past lives. The answer which these individuals receive may have a marked impact on their understanding of self, and thus on the individual and collective reconstruction of autobiography.

Those who are informed by the BStU that they were under Stasi observation and who view their files have often emphasised the importance of subsequently being able to confirm that their personal conception of the biographical details of their life is valid. After accessing his files, Jürgen Fuchs, for example, was finally able to prove that he was in fact arrested, interrogated and practically forced to leave the GDR in the late 1970s (I-36, p. 280). When he was literally abandoned in West Berlin in 1977, Fuchs's memory was the only witness to these events. Fuchs was able to align the Stasi's depiction of his detainment and deportation with his understanding of his own biography. Wolf Biermann also talked of the positive side of viewing one's Stasi files, describing his joy at finding a letter in his file which his mother had sent to him in 1969 but which he had never received (I-47, p. 45).

Information available to an individual who was observed by the Stasi cannot, however, always be incorporated into a pre-existing notion of personal history, but forces its complete re-evaluation, as in the notorious case of Knud and Vera Wollenberger. Had the files been destroyed before her husband's Stasi past had been brought to light, it is conceivable that Vera Wollenberger (now Lengsfeld) might have forever remained ignorant of her husband's activities. Her conception of personal history would, therefore, have always been based on false premises. One might argue that this situation would have been ultimately preferable to the harsh truths Lengsfeld was forced to face. In light of the actual or potentially destructive consequences of accessing the information contained in the files, Lutz Rathenow claimed that viewing these documents had a more profound effect on his life than any other event, including the fall of the Berlin Wall (I-62). Even Joachim Gauck himself admits to skimming over sections of his file and advises everyone to consider very carefully whether or not to view these documents (J-17, p. 96).

Since the network of informers was not evenly spread throughout the population but operated on a Focusing Principle, it is almost inevitable that Stasi victims will discover that some of those whom they previously considered close friends were among those who worked as informers. Similarly, it is just as likely that in some cases they will have wrongly suspected others of such activities. Günter Kunert experienced great relief upon discovering that his immediate neighbours had not been spying on him after all: 'That's another truth which can be gained from the files and a reason why they are read and should be read. They don't just condemn fellow citizens, they rehabilitate them too' (J-46, p. 49). For most Stasi victims viewing one's files is thus a process characterised, as Biermann puts it, by both 'disappointment' and '*dis*-illusionment' (I-39, p. 183). This dichotomy is illustrated by an anecdote from the writer Erich Loest. Loest told of how he wrote a letter to a friend telling him that after viewing his Stasi files he now knew for certain that this man had been one of the informers set upon him (H-2). Loest was shocked later to discover that he had suspected the wrong man. The true identity of the informer concerned was that of a much closer friend, whose trust Loest had never questioned. Loest was forced to re-evaluate his biography in light of this discovery. On the one hand, he experiences the disappointment involved in the realisation that he has believed one man to be a good friend, who, it transpires, reported on his activities to the Stasi. Simultaneously, a feeling of '*dis*-illusionment' results upon discovering that he has wrongly suspected an innocent man. The discovery that one has wrongly judged others can itself be a traumatic experience. Irena Kukutz, one of the members of the Women for Peace group, described the disturbing effects of her realisation that she had wrongly suspected some of the other group members of being Stasi informers:

> I've felt incredibly relieved since the Stasi files have been open because my wish from the beginning of 1992 has come true – which is that I was often wrong about people. And I'm also shocked about the fact that there was so much mistrust within me and that was also one of the informers' tasks, to plant mistrust, and I didn't trust a lot of people and believe that we too were diseased, and I had to come to the realisation that my judgement was often wrong and since then I've talked to some women about the fact that I suspected them and that wasn't always easy (F-13, p. 163).

Kukutz's faith in her sense of judgement was thus shaken, and her memories and conception of personal history had to go through a process of re-evaluation in light of the knowledge which the files brought. Günter Kunert also commented on this regrettable consequence of the all-pervasive mistrust which the system fostered:

> In the defeated system we lived in deformed interpersonal relationships and conditions. We did not act freely in casual encounters with others – like with the neighbours. We automatically blocked our reactions, we turned away as soon as a look seemed too curious to us, a question too probing, an interest in us not sufficiently justified. We lived in many respects like oysters (J-46, p. 49).

Once the possibility exists that a person's understanding of their biography is based on false premises, they may feel compelled to adjust it by viewing their Stasi files. However, there is a potentially high price to be paid for taking such a step and in an article entitled, 'The fear of losing some good memories' Rainer Eppelmann remarked that after viewing his Stasi files he considered himself 'wiser but poorer' (I-3).

If they are still unsure as to the identity of the informers whose cover names appear in their files, victims of Stasi observation such as Kukutz and Kunert may apply to have these de-coded. Marinka Körzendörfer, a member of a lesbian church group, describes her decision to apply to do so as follows: 'Just because with some cover names, for example, I thought that it could have been one of two people. Probably in the end it wasn't either of them but a fifth person – and why should I remember the first two incorrectly?' (J-44, p. 28). The Stasi's influence over the lives of these former victims of observation continues then to be considerable, since such individuals may begin to re-remember the past on the basis of the information which has been recorded in the files. This is not only the case for the area of interpersonal relationships, but also for past behaviour. Bärbel Bohley concluded that the fact that the Stasi did not begin observing her until 1982 meant that she had obviously not been sufficiently active in the opposition scene before this time (J-13, p. 45). Bohley seems to accept the Stasi's evaluation of the extent of her opposition activities. Yet it may be the case that Bohley's commitment to opposition activities before 1982 went unnoticed, rather than that this point marked a decisive change in her stance. Marinka Körzendörfer was similarly disappointed to find that the behaviour of her group was occasionally noted as having been 'exemplary' in the Stasi's reports (J-44, p. 26). The written biographical history seems to be being judged here by the two women to have more objectivity and validity than their autobiographical memory. At other times, Körzendörfer rejects the Stasi's evaluation of events and relies on her own memory. She is, for example, annoyed that no police report is to be found of the arrest of eleven members of the group at the celebrations to mark the fortieth anniversary of the liberation of the concentration camp at Ravensbrück. Körzendörfer remembers that the women certainly did cause a public disturbance on this day (ibid.).

Targets of Stasi observation such as Körzendörfer have an ambivalent relationship to the files, as demonstrated by their evaluation of the quasi-biographical account of their lives which is found in these documents: Klaus Schlesinger felt as though he were reading a novel in which he was the protagonist (J-79, p. 30); Vera Wollenberger found it to be a distorted image of her biography (J-108, p. 8); Lutz Rathenow felt that it was not quite his biography (I-65); and Jürgen Fuchs described it as a perverse and destructive caricature of his (I-72). On the one hand, the Stasi victims reject much of what is written in the files as presenting a twisted or simply inaccurate version of events, yet, on the other, hope that these same documents will be able to help them reconstruct the past and are angered and disappointed to discover that the information available does not always allow them to do so. Körzendörfer, for example, is disappointed to find that some of the group's pamphlets are not to be found in the files: 'I had hoped so much that they would be. Our sense that we should record things for history was not very well developed at that time' (J-44, p. 27). Indeed, Körzendörfer continues: 'Much of what I had hoped to find in the files wasn't there' (ibid.). It is as though she has been hoping that the files will be able to fill in the gaps in her biographical understanding, to make it whole. In actuality the information in the files often does not complete but rather shatters the individual's understanding of personal history.

It is not merely victims of Stasi observation whose understanding of self and biography can be radically altered by the information contained in the files, but also that of those who carried out this surveillance, the unofficial employees. As discussed in previous chapters, many informers report being shocked to discover that they belong to the group of perpetrators. Since the existence of a Stasi file potentially defines the private and public life of former informers, the confrontation with this aspect of an individual's past can potentially result for them not simply in a re-acquisition of their biography, but in its complete redefinition. Informers may wish to view the actual contents of the file and face the choice of whether to apply to do so. If they do decide to take this step, they face certain restrictions on the material which will be made available for viewing. The StUG (§ 16/4) stipulates that informers are only to be granted access to those parts of the files which relate to their person and not to the reports which they helped to compile. This ruling, in addition to the fact that applications from Stasi employees who do apply to see their file are generally not treated with priority, means that many informers have either not seen their files or have been allowed only limited access. Although they often claim that they never reported anything of consequence and cannot be held responsible for causing harm to others, they are really no longer entirely sure of what they said and cannot know how the information they gave was processed and recorded. Almost as though she had been awaiting judgement from the files, 'Stephana' asked me in a state of great excitement after I had viewed her file: 'What sort of person am I then?'. In a similar manner, one of the informers who was reporting on Erich Loest told him that she felt that she could continue to look Loest in the eye, adding, however: 'Or do you perhaps know more about me, do you know anything that I might have forgotten? My thoughts are so confused that it's even possible that I'm deluding myself' (J-52, p. 133).

The dilemma on the part of someone who held contacts with the Stasi of how much to admit to prior to a concrete accusation was particularly evident from the manner in which Manfred Stolpe made his Stasi contacts public. The details of this contact, that Stolpe had met with Stasi officers in secret locations, for example, emerged only gradually during investigations by the Stolpe Committee. Stolpe was only ever prepared to justify those aspects of his Stasi past for which evidence had been produced. Shortly before the final report of the Committee was passed, he claimed to regret the at times lax and ambivalent approach he had taken to making his Stasi contacts public: 'My hesitation has fostered misinterpretation' (I-59). Yet, had Stolpe admitted to all details of the contact in early 1992, he would have been under considerably greater pressure to resign. The course of action he chose was, therefore, the only one which allowed him to remain in office as Premier of Brandenburg.

The writer Sascha Anderson's confrontation with his Stasi past differed from that of Manfred Stolpe's in that the former initially denied having had dealings with the Stasi at all. When he eventually admitted to this fact, Anderson stated that he felt unable to defend himself sufficiently until he had been given the chance to view his files: 'At the moment I'm not in possession of the documents which would allow me to remember the concrete details' (I-79, p. 65). Similarly, 'Wolfgang' told me that he had decided to wait until he had viewed his file before confessing to his family that he had worked as an informer (A-7). 'Wolfgang' is thus, to some extent, waiting for the files to recreate his Stasi biography, the details of which he can no longer be sure of. He is unwilling to tell his family of his work for the Stasi until the files allow him to judge the true extent of his compliance and guilt. Rather as a pupil awaiting a report card might know that they really didn't deserve a good mark, 'Wolfgang' seems to still, like the child, hold out hope that perhaps past misdemeanours will not be too harshly judged. Often, however, it is not the details of an individual's contact to the Stasi upon which judgement by others is based. The label alone of 'unofficial employee' will potentially define the self-perception and public image of those to whom it applies. Informers are often keen to emphasise that their biography should not be defined solely in terms of their previous Stasi connections, and that it is unreasonable that they should be judged only on this one aspect of their past life. 'Sonnenblume', whose contact to the Stasi encompassed a period of just over a year, argued: 'It's only a tiny part of my life after all, just a small part' (A-10). Similarly 'Theodor' feels that no-one understands that his dealings with the Stasi were 'only a small stone in the mosaic of general behaviour' (B-3).

As is true for the victims of Stasi observation, the histories in the files of those who worked as informers allow only a disjointed and fragmented reconstruction of past events. Much is missing, and, consequently, the information which is recorded may be in danger of being retrospectively judged more significant and representative of the individual biography than was the case. For those who know or discover that their behaviour was not sufficiently non-conformist to arouse the Stasi's suspicions and warrant observation, it is the lack of any information on their person in the Stasi's written legacy which forces them to re-evaluate their self-image. At least initially, many were unwilling to face the fact that as opportunistic conformists they had done little to challenge the existing social order. Had the Stasi files been destroyed or not been made available to the public, the self-image of some of those who were neither the agents, nor recipients of direct Stasi observation might have been markedly different, since they could have continued to believe that they had been under surveillance. It was for this reason that Lutz Rathenow argued in 1990 that the Stasi files should be made publicly accessible in order that everyone have the opportunity to assert 'to what extent he was a culprit and to what extent a victim' (J-68, p. 1468). This possibility was subsequently achieved through the Stasi Document Law, and citizens of the former GDR have faced the choice of whether to rely on their existing perception of biography or potentially be forced to completely redefine it in light of the information which is present or absent in these 178 kilometres of filed material.

In the first instance, the Stasi files are significant in that they, albeit often superficially, divide citizens of the former GDR into groups of those who observed, those who were recipients of observation and those who belong to neither of these two categories. This categorisation alone, although there is much differentiation within each grouping, affects the way in which individuals remember and interpret their past. In the years since the law came into force, many have been shocked to learn that there is an absence of any information relating to them in the Stasi files. For those who belong to one of the two minority groups, that is the direct agents or recipients of Stasi observation, the information available potentially has considerable and traumatic impact on their conception of autobiography, in terms of how they view their interpersonal relationships, their own character, and their past behaviour. The lessons of the Stasi files have the potential both to dispel and to create myths about the course of individual and collective biographies in the GDR, and the knowledge which these documents have brought will thus have a profound and lasting impact on the way in which future histories of the German Democratic Republic are written and re-written. In this sense, the Stasi files can be said to recreate the biography of a lost state.

11

IMPACT AND IMPLICATIONS OF AN EXTRAORDINARY LEGACY

In the immediate aftermath of the events surrounding German unification, the Stasi debate was at the forefront of any discussion of the GDR's problematic legacy, leading journalist Peter Jochen Winters to remark: 'At the moment the confrontation with the SED dictatorship consists almost exclusively of tracking down employees of the former GDR's Ministry of State Security' (I-15). Joachim Gauck described the sensational emphasising of this aspect of GDR history as 'Stasi-hysteria', arguing that this tendency was indicative of obvious deficiencies in the approach to the confrontation with the past (I-2). Yet the hysteria and hyperbole which characterised the Stasi debate in its initial stages were arguably inevitable. If East Germans were not already obsessed with the Stasi after having lived their lives imagining that its spies might be just around every corner, then the post-Wall discovery that this system could have nurtured such absurdities as a husband reporting on his own wife only served to increase the macabre fascination of the issue.

In GDR times, the malaise, described by some as a form of schizophrenia, which developed in response to the permanent suspicion that one might be under surveillance, had spread its way so gradually throughout the population that many were unaware that they too had been affected. Once the system which had nurtured it had collapsed, the wounds which it had left were laid bare and soon became the object of much popular and scholarly attention. In addition to the freak appeal which the intricacies of this rather unpleasant side of GDR history held, another key factor in ensuring that the debate concerning Stasi informers remained at the forefront of the reckoning with the recent past was the desire on the part of a people which had been active as both the agents and victims of surveillance to understand the mechanisms which had shaped the course of their past lives. This process involved establishing the identities of the informers which had until then been so well-disguised that it seemed even some informers themselves were unaware that they, too, had worked for the Stasi.

The debate concerning informers received extensive media coverage, but it was not the case that those engaged in the confrontation with the GDR past were solely concerned with this issue. In Bonn, an Enquete Commission was being set up to examine various aspects and consequences of the dictatorship. Around the same time, the question of how the crimes of leading Party functionaries should be addressed within the legal system was causing some commotion. The former head of state, Erich Honecker, was eventually ordered out of his refuge in the Chilean embassy in Moscow and brought back to Berlin for trial. The attempt to bring Honecker to justice was farcical from its outset, as were many such undertakings concerning prominent Party members. These men had managed to assume important functions in the GDR up until the point of its demise. Yet immediately, and perhaps plausibly, after the events of 1989–90, their health had apparently taken a severe turn for the worse. Consequently, any judicial proceedings were greatly hindered by constant pleas that the accused were medically unfit for trial. Eventually, the trial against Honecker was abandoned and, although it was suspected that the severity of his ailing condition had been exaggerated, these doubting voices were silenced when, after being released and having settled in Chile with his wife and daughter, the old man did, indeed, die of the cancer he had complained of throughout the trial. Attempts to bring Erich Mielke to court were also the subject of much interest, as were proceedings against various border-guards, the latter amounting to a lengthy series of trials headed by the fraught determination of Karin Gueffroy to see that justice be done for the death of her son Chris in February 1989. The nineteen-year-old waiter from Berlin had been the last person to be killed while trying to flee West.

As sensational as the above events were, they did not touch the individuals who were not immediately affected by them to quite the same extent as the discussion regarding Stasi informers. Until material from the files became available this was a phenomenon which potentially reached into the most intimate sphere of every last East German. Focusing on this particular aspect of the GDR's legacy was also conceptually easier, since the Stasi was a historical entity which it seemed possible to define and analyse. A true examination of the historical and political factors which had shaped the course of events in East Germany could only really have taken place within the context of an analysis of the recent past within, between and beyond the two Germanys. Such an undertaking was not only vast, but also one which, for example, few of those in positions of power in the former FRG were keen to embark on. The trials involving those who had acted as mediators between East and West, such as the lawyer Wolfgang Vogel, and Alexander Schalck-Golodkowski, the head of the GDR's money laundering body, euphemistically named Commercial Co-ordination, were already sufficiently uncomfortable. The informer debate was also a more accessible one for the ordinary person, since it seemed not to be an abstract legal or political discussion, but one concerning the most basic of interpersonal issues, such as trust and betrayal.

After the elation of unification had subsided, former East Germans soon became aware that, although they could now travel outside the GDR without further ado, and had access to the so-longed-for consumer goods, these freedoms had only been attained at a price. Despite the boom industry of the numerous re-training programmes established in the immediate post-unification period, unemployment figures began to rise dramatically in the former East. The loss of the material security which had been taken so much for granted in the GDR was experienced as an unpleasant and unexpected shock for many East Germans who had been dazzled by the neon glitter of the West. Stefan Heym observed that the East Germans had hoped for socialism and luxurious department stores after unification and had got in their place unemployment and no-name supermarkets (I-85). Former East Germans, previously relatively affluent in the Eastern Bloc, now found themselves in a socially and materially inferior position to those in the FRG. Overnight, they had become children in their own country who had to be re-trained and re-educated to the ways of the West. Hans-Joachim Maaz remarked that, whereas at first East Germans had embraced and idealised West German culture, a period of 'sobering up, disappointment and embittered disillusionment' had begun to set in as the full scale of the economic consequences could no longer be disguised (J-53, p. 33). In retrospect, the distinct advantages of life under the umbrella of the socialist dictatorship which had been so gladly forsaken began to seem increasingly attractive. The unaccustomed burden of social and material concerns resulted in the first signs of nostalgia for the lost state, and a period of mourning for this loss set in, leading Biermann to observe: 'It stinks of self-pity in the East' (J-11, p. 141).

This nostalgia, popularly referred to as Eastalgia, resulted primarily from a sense of loss of the security and familiarity of life in the GDR. It seemed that almost every aspect of former life had been replaced by the system which had been in force in the FRG. East Germans experienced this course of events as signifying that all they had learned in the GDR, and therefore their whole lives, had been worthless. Several of those with whom I spoke mentioned the frustration and disillusionment they felt at having, as they expressed it, lived a substantial proportion of their lives in vain. Former Stasi informers will often tend to experience this feeling more acutely than those whose past history is not so potentially incriminating, but the sentiment was indicative of a general mood. Often the perceived arrogance of the West was seen as being at the root of this problem, as the following words from 'Theodor' illustrate:

> As a result of the speed with which unification was realised we've really been put on the defensive and we have to defend things – I catch myself at it sometimes – defending things which I used to curse at – simply because the ignorance about makes me furious. That's a really dangerous tendency (A-2).

Michael Schmitz addressed the issue of why, in psychological terms, it was unrealistic to expect that those in the East would do anything but defend the system they, however willingly or unwillingly, had lived in:

> He who expects former East Germans to concede that their whole life in the GDR was a waste of time, forces them to defend the old regime, because if they did not do this they would be denying their own self (I-57, p. 40).

Yet, unification was not forced upon the former GDR. A majority had initially embraced it and merrily discarded the restraints of their previous life. Later, a mourning process began for this loss, intensified by the realisation that public and private identity had been integrally linked with and dependent on a social reality which had so rapidly and almost entirely disappeared. Margarete Mitscherlich, whose analysis of the way in which ordinary Germans coped with the end of the National Socialist dictatorship had such an impact in the Federal Republic, compared the conclusions which she had made then regarding former West Germans with the situation of East Germans after 1989:

> The mourning for the Hitler period has up until now, as far as concerns us, been above all a mourning for the loss of one's individual or group ideal and one's self- or group-esteem. I think that this is a feeling which is shared by many countrymen from the former GDR as regards unification (J-58, p. 413).

The upsurge of these feelings of self-pity and nostalgia were not indications that the average East German truly desired the resurrection of the SED state, merely that they experienced the need to regain a sense of self which had disappeared with it. A sense of common identity began to develop which was partly based on fact and partly on retrospective sentimentality:

> You'll never understand that! is the defence mechanism with which the inhabitants of the GDR protect their self-pity and at the same time attempt, with the aid of such a right to memory, to preserve their identity and heal themselves (J-51, p. 27).

Joachim Gauck referred to this focusing on the past as a desire for 'the sweet poison of dependency' and bemoaned the fact that many East Germans were unwilling to come to terms with the freedom they so had wished for (I-76). Instead, they yearned for the days when they could, under the dictatorship, enjoy the security offered to them by their role as the legitimate objects of decision-making, dependent on the state to determine every aspect of their lives.

The perceived victimisation of East Germans, and perceived criminalisation of the structures which had supported the GDR, meant then that many felt that their entire previous life had been negated. They found themselves sharing a common fate with those whom they would have previously considered adversaries, and the Stasi informer no longer constituted the greatest evil in this new society. In addition, accounts of how brutal life under the dictatorship had been were no longer so popularly received, since a true confrontation with the crimes of the former regime did not facilitate indulgence in the nostalgia which had become so prevalent. At the same time as few were keen to be reminded of the harsher aspects of life in the GDR, many excused their previous lack of nonconformist behaviour with the reasoning that conditions had been so oppressive that they had been faced with no real alternative but to comply:

> Their [former East Germans] justification arguments reveal inconsistencies. They maintain that the way they are being treated now by the West Germans is much worse than was the case under the old regime; in the same breath they explain that the dictatorship squashed every deviation from the norm to such an extent that there was really no alternative but to fully conform (I-57, p. 40).

The small minority of those who had made their criticisms audible in the GDR, and who subsequently suffered for doing so, were left feeling embittered as they realised that they were among a dwindling minority interested in an extensive confrontation with the past. Their situation was, to some extent, comparable to that of victims of Nazi persecution, some of whom narrowly escaped death in camps only to find that no one was particularly interested in hearing their tales of horror. This parallelism of experience is noted by Jürgen Fuchs, who quotes Viktor Frankl, a concentration camp survivor, to illustrate the point:

> When someone like that returns home and comes to realise that he is met everywhere with nothing but people shrugging their shoulders or uttering empty words, a bitterness often takes hold of him which forces him to ask himself why it was that he actually went through it all (J-27, pp. 81–2).

In the immediate post-Wall period, when it seemed that a victimised population had freed itself from its malignant oppressor, culprits were sought who had been instrumental in enforcing a system of control so brutal that it had allowed almost no resistance. The Stasi files, it appeared initially, would serve to identify these individuals. After these had been secured, primarily through the efforts of various grass roots groups, many in the East were keen to feast on their contents:

> We owe it to the commitment of courageous people in the citizens' rights movement that most of the Stasi files were saved from destruction and from being arrogantly used by West German authorities and archives. This was one of the few victories left over from the 'revolution' which wasn't actually a revolution. The right to view one's Stasi files, which was laboriously pushed through despite the desire for general amnesty and for hasty forgetting, expressed above all in the West, has also seemed until now to be a left-over chance to be able to clarify and sort out our own affairs after all. Yet, this hope is fading more and more. These files are increasingly being used to hunt down scapegoats rather than to determine guilt and entanglement in abnormal social relations (J-55, p. 81).

Soon it became evident that these scapegoats were not so easy to define, that it had been a small minority who could claim to be bona fide Stasi victims. These victims now served only to remind the majority of their own lack of active resistance and of the brutality of a system which they wished to idealise retrospectively. Once again, the comparison to the immediate post-war period was apt, as demonstrated by the following statement from Ruth Klüger describing the cold reception concentration camp survivors such as herself received at this time: 'Simply by being there the survivors reminded others of the past and what had gone on there' (J-42, p. 196).

In the hot-pot of deception, secrecy, and lies which the Stasi files promised, it had seemed at first that informers made up a definable group who were more obviously guilty than the majority. Individual tales soon emerged from the files, however, underlining the fact that the informer was not a type, but that many different individuals had become involved with the Stasi in this way for a variety of circumstantial reasons.

The paradox of the system which had seen many informers working with the opposition at the same time as they worked against it continued to be a feature of the post-unification period. Werner Sellhorn, editor of the magazine Listen and Watch, a publication concerned solely with the confrontation with the GDR past, was unmasked, for example, as having worked as a Stasi informer. Indeed, there were many surprises regarding those who had or had not conspired with the Stasi. The Focusing Principle meant that a significant proportion of those who had been in some way active in the opposition had themselves worked for the Stasi. The cases of individuals such as Sascha Anderson, Manfred Stolpe, and even Christa Wolf served only to blur further the boundaries of relative culpability. A form of re-humanisation of the individuals behind the label 'unofficial employee' took place, since it was clear that levels of guilt between any two cases could vary significantly. It was recognised that a differentiated approach to each individual case was required which would ideally take into account not only the specific details of the case, but also the societal context, including an analysis of the roles which others not necessarily classified by the Stasi as unofficial employees had played in the mechanisms of control. Such a mass moral reckoning was, however, never feasible, given the strains of unification, and a discernible lack of desire to engage in it. The fact that the system had not been reformed, but completely obliterated, ensured that any comprehensive legal confrontation with the crimes of the past would be extremely complicated. Furthermore, the individual or collective guilt of individual informers often defied definition in a legal context. Although informers had not been physically omnipresent, they had helped to create a general atmosphere of distrust and secrecy which had ensured that many a critical sentiment was never voiced lest it should be reported to higher powers. This prevailing air of caution and fear also contributed to the fact that much opposition activity remained in the underground, surfacing only in the very latter days of the GDR's existence. The Stasi's informers had been an extremely important part of the machinery, but these mechanisms could never have functioned without the silent conformity of the vast majority of East Germans. As opportunistic conformists, individuals complied with the collective because they had become comfortable in the slumber of a predictable pattern of material and social security, in which the individual's true convictions were subordinated to the desire for a simple and relatively harmonious life.

In this turbulent climate, and despite initial resistance to its implementation, it is in many ways a miracle that the Stasi Document Law has stood the test of time. Thousands of applications to view files continue to flood into the BStU, and the man at the head of this institution, Joachim Gauck, describes the continued existence of these files and the confrontation with their contents as a medicine against nostalgia, believing that without them 'the lies of those who used to be in power would be considerably greater, as would the degree of retrospective glorification in large parts of the population' (I-20). Although nostalgia for the GDR has managed to blossom despite the shadow of the files, they have certainly had a traumatic impact. The detailed accounts of past lives which are found there have brought shock revelations, and individuals have been forced to reassess their biography in the light of this newly-acquired knowledge. This re-evaluation has resulted in the often unwelcome acknowledgement that a proportion of what any one individual assumed about their past life in the GDR may be invalid. This shock, along with the numerous other strains resulting from unification, hit a population which was, for the most part, quite unprepared for its intensity.

Any truly differentiated confrontation with the GDR past was never going to be achieved when East Germans, particularly former Stasi informers, felt that their social and material existence was seriously threatened and that they were in danger of losing hold of an individual and a collective identity. The wide-scale societal confrontation with the Stasi legacy was, at least in the years immediately following unification, hectic, sensational, and mostly undifferentiated. Any debate within the former East was, furthermore, clouded by the shadow of the West, the other, socially and materially dominant Germany. Joachim Gauck prophesied that it would take two generations for the citizens of former East Germany to liberate themselves from the 'subordinate mentality' which, in forty years of the GDR's existence, had so gradually worked its way into the population (I-34). During the passing of these next two generations most former East Germans will be very much more concerned with integration into the new societal structures. Yet, after the passing of this time, a rebellion similar to that which occurred in the FRG in 1968 is unlikely, if it were to result at all, to have a similar impact to that of the angry post-war generation in the former FRG: first, since the events of the late 1960s were not particular to

Germany, only their specific content; and second, since some form of public debate has taken place regarding the most recent past, necessitated by the unique decision to make the Stasi files publicly available. This decision was, moreover, taken as a result of the pressure applied from within the former GDR. Some of the decisive policy-making regarding dealings with this unique legacy was, therefore, in contrast to the immediate post-war period, fought out by those who were directly involved and not by a foreign and victorious power. Finally, and perhaps most significantly, although there is no doubt that severe injustices were committed under SED rule, in extreme cases resulting in death or lifelong physical and/or psychological injury, these atrocities are quite simply not comparable in their mass and brutality to the crimes of National Socialism, and, therefore, not the focus of the same degree of international attention. Erich Honecker and his Politburo had stood by and watched their order to shoot be executed and had overseen the often harsh suppression of any anti-government activities detected by its internal security organ, but theirs is a crime which simply does not have the same resonance as the attempted extermination of entire social and religious groups.

In the meantime, those whose specified task it was to ensure that the implicit and explicit mechanisms of control which supported the system were maintained, that is the informers, are often seen as carrying a greater proportion of at least moral guilt than those who were much farther up the power hierarchy. Some of these informers quite genuinely feel no regret in relation to their past actions. Most, however, must live with the real or threatened stigma and shame of having engaged in such dishonourable activity in the service of a defeated and corrupt power. This is a crime which has been distinguished from other forms of compliance within East Germany, in that merely the label 'unofficial employee' can potentially result in being socially ostracised and suffering material loss. Many informers thus stand judged guilty of a crime which often defies legal definition in anything other than the name, and awaiting a punishment which may or may not follow.

The detailed accounts of past lives in the GDR which are found in the Stasi files have brought both welcome and unwelcome surprises, and individuals have been forced to reassess their personal history in the light of this newly-acquired knowledge. The histories of collectives such as the GDR Writers' Association must, too, be rethought and rewritten to incorporate the information contained in the files. It has, for example, been established that in 1987, a staggering twelve of the nineteen committee members of the Writers' Association were active as Stasi informers. (I-58, p. 225; J-100, p. 558). The files do not merely help the people of the former GDR to acquire and understand their own history, but, to a certain extent force its re-definition. Even some of those who were under Stasi observation are traumatised by the realisation that significant details of their perception of the past, in terms particularly of interpersonal relationships, but also of past behaviour, may have been based on false premises. This re-definition of personal and collective history is the true and far-reaching impact of the turbulent confrontation with this aspect of the extraordinary legacy of the GDR's Ministry for State Security, the Stasi.

GLOSSARY

ABBREVIATIONS

AfNS Office for National Security. Before it was eventually disbanded, the Stasi was initially to be reformed and was renamed the AfNS.

AIM Shelved file for an unofficial employee who was no longer active for the Stasi.

ASt District office.

BStU The Office of the Federal Commissioner for the Files of the State Security Service of the former German Democratic Republic, popularly referred to as the Gauck Office.

CDU Christian Democratic Union.

FDJ Free German Youth Group.

FDP Free Democratic Party.

FIM Unofficial employee in charge of other unofficial employees.

FRG Federal Republic of Germany. West Germany.

GDR German Democratic Republic. East Germany.

GMS A person who periodically supplied the Stasi with information but to whom contact was less formalised and less secretive than to an unofficial employee.

GVS Secret document.

HFIM Unofficial employee in charge of other unofficial employees. Whereas FIM continued in their regular employment after commencing work for the Stasi, HFIMs worked for the Stasi on a full-time basis and often had a cover occupation.

HVA The Stasi's foreign espionage department.

IM Unofficial employee – the term used by the Stasi for its informers.

IMB Unofficial employees who were directly assigned to observe specific individuals suspected of enemy activity.

IME Unofficial employees recruited for a specific purpose.

IMS Unofficial employees involved in the effective penetration and safeguarding of the designated area of operation.

IMV Earlier term for an IMB.

JHS Stasi College located near Potsdam.

MfS Ministry for State Security – the official name for the Stasi.

OPK Initital Stasi surveillance measure which had three main applications: to confirm or reject suspicions that an individual had acted unlawfully; to identify individuals who were negatively disposed towards the state; and to screen individuals who held positions of power which were potentially open to misuse. An OPK sometimes led to an OV.

OV The next and more intensive stage of surveillance after an OPK. Informers were to establish or to exploit already existing contacts to individuals who were being observed under an OV, so aiming to obtain information which was of 'operative significance'.

PDS Party of Democratic Socialism – the follow-on party from the SED.

SED Socialist Unity Party – the ruling party in the GDR.

SPD Social Democratic Party.

Stasi More popular term for the MfS.

StUG Stasi Document Law.

VVS Confidential document.

ZA Central archive.

COMMON TERMS

Candidate An individual who the Stasi intended to recruit as an informer if thorough checks carried out on the person and their family proved satisfactory.

Contact Meeting The initial meeting between the candidate and the Stasi.

Eastalgia Popular term referring to nostalgia for the GDR.

Enquete Commission Commission set up in 1992 which was concerned with examining and documenting the history and consequences of SED rule in the GDR. Its work included inviting individuals before the commission to testify on various aspects of life under the dictatorship, and commissioning reports from researchers working in the field. The final report of this Enquete Commission was passed in June 1994.

Focusing Principle Working principle of the Stasi, whereby resources were not to be distributed evenly among the population but concentrated in areas of suspected subversive activity.

Gauck Office The more popular term for the office of the BStU, named after the head of the organisation, Joachim Gauck.

Legend The term used for the pretexts used by the Stasi in all aspects of its work.

Oath of Silence The (usually written) oath which informers in the process of being recruited were asked to make at the end of the Contact Meeting.

Order to Shoot The order to shoot anyone found trying to leave the GDR illegally. The exact implications of the Order to Shoot, i.e., whether it had been an order to kill or merely to wound, were heavily debated in the controversial series of border-guard trials.

Personal File The volume(s) of informers' files, in which their personal details were recorded alongside any information relating to their immediate family. Documentation regarding the selection and recruitment of informers was also stored here, as well as other general information, such as any rewards received for services rendered.

Pioneers The state-run organisation for children in the GDR, of which membership was an implicit duty.

Requirement Profile A Requirement Profile defined a particular task, and identified, in terms of experience, ability and personality, the type of person who might be suitable for it and who, therefore, could potentially be recruited as an informer.

Round Table The body set up in the immediate post-Wall period to facilitate inter-party dialogue in the transition period of the run-up to the first and last democratic elections in the GDR in March 1990.

Statement of Commitment The (usually written) declaration of commitment which newly-recruited informers were asked to make at recruitment.

Stolpe Committee Parliamentary committee set up in 1992 to clarify the nature and extent of Manfred Stolpe's Stasi connections.

Treuhand Body set up to administer the privatisation of formerly state-run GDR businesses and properties.

Unofficial Employee The Stasi's official term for the informers they engaged.

Work File The volume(s) of informers' files where the actual reports of the meetings between the informers and the officer(s) in charge of the case were filed.

KEY PERSONALITIES

Biermann, Wolf (b. 1936) Singer and songwriter. Refused re-entry to the GDR in 1976 after being allowed out to perform in West Germany.

Bohley, Bärbel (b. 1945) Citizens' rights campaigner in the GDR. Arrested in January 1988 after protesting at the Rosa-Luxemburg Demonstration. Temporarily left the GDR soon afterwards to escape a long jail sentence. Involved in various opposition/peace groups such as the Initiative for Peace and Human Rights.

Böhme, Ibrahim (b. 1938) Co-founder of the *SDP* (the East German SPD in the immediate post-Wall period), Stasi informer.

De Maizière, Lothar (b. 1940) Leader of the GDR from April–October 1990, Stasi informer.

Eigenfeld, Katrin (b. 1946) Citizens' rights campaigner in the GDR. Active in various church/peace groups. Co-founder of the Neues Forum Party in Halle.

Eppelmann, Rainer (b. 1943) Citizens' rights campaigner in the GDR and theologian. Chairman (CDU) of the Enquete Commission.

Fuchs, Jürgen (b. 1950) Writer and psychologist. Close acquaintance of Robert Havemann. Arrested in 1976 after protest at Wolf Biermann's expulsion. Forced to leave the GDR in 1977 after nine months imprisonment.

Gauck, Joachim (b. 1940) Federal Commissioner in charge of the Stasi files.

Gysi, Gregor (b. 1948) Lawyer and politician (PDS).

Havemann, Robert (1910–1982) Physicist and possibly the most prominent East German dissident. Placed under constant surveillance and banned from leaving his home by the Stasi.

Honecker, Erich (1912–1994) Leader of the SED from 1976–1989.

Mielke, Erich (b. 1907) Minister for State Security from 1957–1989.

Nooke, Günter (b. 1959) Citizens' rights campaigner in the GDR. Representative of Bündnis 90 (later Bündnis) on the Stolpe Committee.

Poppe, Gerd (b. 1941) Citizens' rights campaigner in the GDR. Co-founder of the Initiative for Peace and Human Rights.

Poppe, Ulrike (b. 1953) Citizens' rights campaigner in the GDR. Founding member of the Women for Peace group.

Rathenow, Lutz (b. 1952) Writer and citizens' rights campaigner in the GDR. Active in literary circles in Jena in the 1970s and 1980s.

Reich, Jens (b. 1939) Biologist and citizens' rights campaigner in the GDR. MP for Alliance 90/The Greens after the first and last free elections in the GDR (March–October 1990).

Schnur, Wolfgang (b. 1944) Lawyer in the GDR, Stasi informer.

Schorlemmer, Friedrich (b. 1944) Theologian. Formerly regarded as belonging to the group of prominent citizens' rights campaigners. In the years after unification, increasingly distanced himself from this group as he was not in agreement with the stance they took on dealings with the Stasi legacy.

Stolpe, Manfred (b. 1936) Leading church functionary in the GDR. Premier (SPD) of Brandenburg since 1990.

Wolf, Markus (b. 1923) Head of the HVA, the Stasi's foreign espionage department.

Wollenberger (now Lengsfeld), Vera (b. 1952) Citizens' rights campaigner in the GDR. Arrested in January 1988 after protesting at the Rosa-Luxemburg Demonstration. Temporarily left the GDR soon afterwards to escape a long jail sentence.

Wollweber, Ernst (1898–1967) Secretary of State and then Minister for State Security (1953–1957).

Zaisser, Wilhelm (1893–1958) Minister for State Security from 1950–1953.

BIBLIOGRAPHY

A. INTERVIEWS WITH FORMER STASI INFORMERS

1. 'Rolf': Interview with the author on 29 October 1994.
2. 'Theodor': Interview with the author on 8 November 1994.
3. 'Falke': Interview with the author on 14 November 1994.
4. 'Reiner': Interview with the author on 26 November 1994.
5. 'Thaer': Interview with the author on 28 November 1994.
6. 'Fuchs': Interview with the author on 12 December 1994 .
7. 'Wolfgang': Interview with the author on 19 December 1994.
8. 'Stephana': Interview with the author on 19 January 1995.
9. 'Katrin': Interview with the author on 3 March 1995.
10. 'Sonnenblume': Interview with the author on 22 March 1995.

B. CORRESPONDENCE

1. 'Rolf': Letter to the author, 26 February 1995.
2. 'Theodor': Letter to the author, 9 October 1994.
3. 'Theodor': Letter to the author, 29 March 1995.
4. 'Falke': Letter to 'Falke' from the Ministry of the Interior, 28 December 1993.
5. 'Thaer': Letter to the author from the Public Prosecutor, 27 June 1995.
6. 'Fuchs': Letter to the Ministry of Justice, 30 March 1994.
7. 'Fuchs': Letter to the author, 31 October 1995.

C. STASI FILES

1a. 'Rolf': BStU, ASt. Halle, AIM 1223/89, Personal File.
b. 'Rolf': BStU, ASt. Halle, AIM 1223/89, Work File.
2a. 'Theodor': BStU, ZA, AIM 5665/85, Personal File, 2 vols.
b. 'Theodor': BStU, ZA, AIM 5665/85, Work File.
3a. 'Falke': BStU, ASt. Potsdam, Reg.-Nr. IV 922/77, Personal File.
b. 'Falke': BStU, ASt. Potsdam, Reg.-Nr. IV 922/77, Work File, 2 vols.
4a. 'Reiner': BStU, ASt. Potsdam, Reg.-Nr. IV 285/70, Personal File, 2 vols.
b. 'Reiner': BStU, ASt. Potsdam, Reg.-Nr. IV 285/70, Work File, 3 vols.
5a. 'Fuchs': BStU, ASt. Potsdam, Reg.-Nr. IV 0060/77, Personal File.
b. 'Fuchs': BStU, ASt. Potsdam, Reg.-Nr. IV 0060/77, Work File.
6a. 'Stephana': BStU, ASt. Potsdam, Reg.-Nr. IV 1709/85, Personal File.
b. 'Stephana': BStU, ASt. Potsdam, Reg.-Nr. IV 1709/85, Work File, 2 vols.
7a. 'Katrin': BStU, ZA, AIM 5220/88, Personal File.
b. 'Katrin': BStU, ZA, AIM 5220/88, Work File.
8a. 'Sonnenblume': BStU, ASt. Erfurt, AIM 2065/80, Personal File.
b. 'Sonnenblume': BStU, ASt. Erfurt, AIM 2065/80, Work File.

D. STASI DOCUMENTATION

1. Edelmann, Oberst Professor, 'Operativ bedeutsame Informationen und die politisch-operative Einschätzung von Informationen' (JHS, 1985) VVS-o001: JHS 80/85.
2. Gellert, OSL Dr., 'Grundfragen der Wahrung und Erhöhung der Konspiration, Geheimhaltung und Wachsamkeit in der Arbeit mit den Inoffiziellen Mitarbeitern und der Gestaltung einer sicheren Verbindung zwischen dem MfS und den Inoffiziellen Mitarbeitern' (JHS, 1984) VVS-o001: JHS 117/84.
3. Gellert, OSL Dr., 'Die Gewinnung qualifizierter IM – ein objektives Erfordernis zur weiteren Erhöhung der sicherheitspolitischen Wirksamkeit der politisch-operativen Arbeit' (JHS, 1984) VVS-o001: JHS 135/84.
4. Korth, W., Jonak, F., and Scharbert, K.-O., 'Die Gewinnung Inoffizieller Mitarbeiter und ihre psychologischen Bedingungen', 2 vols. (JHS, 1973) VVS MfS 160 – 800/73: JHS 21826.
5. Kotira, M., 'Grundfragen der politisch-ideologischen und tschekistischen Erziehung und Befähigung der IM und der Formung und Entwicklung ihres Feindbildes' (JHS, 1984) VVS-o001: JHS 118/84.
6. Seidler, W. and Schmidt, E., 'Die Rolle der Übereinstimmung zwischen gesellschaftlichen Interessen und den Interessen der Individuen als Triebkraft der Tätigkeit Inoffizieller Mitarbeiter des MfS: Die Notwendigkeit der systematischen Entwicklung dieser Triebkraft in der inoffiziellen Zusammenarbeit und die Aufgaben der Mitarbeiter des MfS, diese Triebkraft gegen die Feinde des Sozialismus zur vollen Wirkung zu bringen', 2 vols. (JHS, 1968) GVS MfS 160 – 53/68: JHS 21782.
7. Wardezki, G., 'Die Dokumentation und Auswertung operativ bedeutsamer Informationen zu IM – eine wesentliche Grundlage für die Erhöhung der Wirksamkeit des IM-Systems', 2 vols (JHS, 1972) GVS MfS 160 – 253/72: JHS 21813.
8. 'Probleme der Entwicklung und Einschätzung von Vertrauensverhältnissen

zwischen inoffiziellen und operativen Mitarbeitern' (JHS, 1979) VVS-o001: JHS 37/79.

9. 'Die Kontaktierung des IM-Kandidaten' (JHS, 1985) VVS-o001: JHS 1/85.
10. 'Ausgewählte Probleme der Treffvorbereitung, -durchführung und -auswertung' (JHS, 1988) VVS-o001: JHS 93/88.
11. 'Material zur Auswertung eines auf Tonträger aufgenommenen Treffgesprächs mit einem IM' (JHS, 1988) VVS-o001: JHS 115/88.

E. SED ARCHIVES

1. 'Bericht über Republikfluchten von Bürgern des demokratischen Sektors Berlin nach Westberlin, die entweder von Angehörigen des MfS angesprochen wurden, oder mit denselben bereits in Verbindung standen' (SAPMO – Party Archive) DY 30 IV 2/12/109 .

F. ADDITIONAL PRIMARY DOCUMENTATION

1. *Bericht der Enquete-Komission: 'Aufarbeitung von Geschichte und Folgen der SED-Diktatur in Deutschland'*, ed. Deutscher Bundestag, 12/7820. Bonn: 1994.
2. *Bericht des Untersuchungsasuschusses 1/3*, 1/3009, 3 vols. Brandenburg: Landtag Brandenburg, 1994.
3. *Das Wörterbuch der Staatssicherheit: Definitionen des MfS zur 'politisch-operativen Arbeit'*, ed. BStU, Series A, 1/1993. Berlin: BStU, 1993 [this material can also be found in the *Wörterbuch der Staatssicherheit: Definitionen zur politisch-operativen Arbeit*, ed. Suckut, S. Berlin: Ch. Links, 1996].
4. *Die Inoffiziellen Mitarbeiter*, ed. BStU, Series B, 3/1993. Berlin: BStU, 1993.
5. *Die Inoffiziellen Mitarbeiter: Richtlinien, Befehle, Direktiven*, ed. BStU, Series A, 1/1992, 2 vols. Berlin: BStU, 1992.
6. *Duell im Dunkeln – Spionage und Gegenspionage im geteilten Deutschland: Veranstaltung der Alternativen Enquête-Kommission Deutsche Zeitgeschichte am 29. Mai 1994 im Berliner Ensemble*, ed. Insider-Komitee zur Aufarbeitung der Geschichte des MfS, IK-Korr Spezial 3. Berlin: Insider-Komitee, 1994.
7. Engelmann, R., *Zu Struktur, Charakter und Bedeutung der Unterlagen des Ministeriums für Staatssicherheit*, ed. BStU, BF informiert, 3/1994. Berlin: BStU, 1994.
8. *Erster Tätigkeitsbericht des Bundesbeauftragten für die Unterlagen des Staatssicherheitsdienstes der ehemaligen Deutschen Demokratischen Republik*. Berlin: BStU, 1993.
9. *Forum zur Aufklärung und Erneuerung* [documentation published with the constitution, passed on 22 March 1992 in Leipzig].
10. Müller-Enbergs, H., *IM-Statistik 1985–1989*, BF informiert, 3/1993. Berlin: BStU, 1993.
11. Müller-Enbergs, H., *Normative Grundlagen des MfS für die Arbeit mit Inoffiziellen Mitarbeitern: Eine Dokumentation* [expertise compiled for the *Enquete-Komission des Deutschen Bundestages zur 'Aufarbeitung von Geschichte und Folgen der SED-Diktatur in Deutschland'*, 1994].
12. Noelle-Neumann, Professor Dr. E., *Vergangenheitsbewältigung: Selbstgespräch und Wir-Gefühl in den neuen Bundesländern*. Allensbach: Institut für Demoskopie, 1992.

13. Protocol of the 23rd Sitting of the *Enquete-Kommission: 'Aufarbeitung von Geschichte und Folgen der SED-Diktatur in Deutschland'*, on *'Das ehemalige Ministerium für Staatssicherheit'*, 15 January 1993, ed. Deutscher Bundestag. Bonn: 1993.
14. Protocol of the 68th Sitting of the *Enquete-Kommission: 'Aufarbeitung von Geschichte und Folgen der SED-Diktatur in Deutschland'*, on *'Motivationen, Möglichkeiten und Grenzen widerständigen und oppositionellen Verhaltens'*, 16 March 1994, ed. Deutscher Bundestag. Bonn: 1994.
15. Protocol of the *Debatte zum Bericht des Parlamentarischen Untersuchungsausschusses 1/3 des Landtages: 'Aufklärung der früheren Kontakte des Ministerpräsidenten Dr. Manfred Stolpe zu Organisationen des Staatsapparates der DDR der SED sowie zum Staatssicherheitsdienst und der in diesem Zusammenhang erhobenen Vorwürfe'*, 16 June 1994, Schriften des Landtages Brandenburg, 2 (1994).
16. *Veröffentlichte Gesetzmaterialien des Parlamentsarchivs* 24. Bonn: Wissenschaftliche Dienste des deutschen Bundestages, 1992.
17. *Zweiter Tätigkeitsbericht des Bundesbeauftragten für die Unterlagen des Staatssicherheitsdienstes der ehemaligen Deutschen Demokratischen Republik*. Berlin: BStU, 1995.

G. LAWS

1. 'Rechtsverhältnisse der Arbeitnehmer im öffentlichen Dienst' (*Bundesgesetzblatt 1990*, Kapitel XIX, Anlage I, Abschnitt III, 1. (5)).
2. *Gesetz über die Sicherung und Nutzung der personenbezogenen Daten des ehemaligen Ministeriums für Staatssicherheit/Amt für Nationale Sicherheit* (*DDR-Gesetzblatt 1990*).
3. *Gesetz über die Unterlagen des Staatssicherheitsdienstes der ehemaligen Deutschen Demokratischen Republik (Stasi-Unterlagen-Gesetz, StUG)*, (*Bundesgestzblatt 1991*, Section I, pp. 2272–87).

H. PUBLIC DISCOURSE

1. 'Täter/Opfer' discussion evening, Haus am Checkpoint Charlie, 2 March 1992 [from video-tapes, viewed with the kind permission of Christina von Camstein, Haus am Checkpoint Charlie].
2. Conference organised by the *Bürgerkomitee Leipzig für die Auflösung der Staatssicherheit*, 'Einblick in das Herrschaftswissen einer Diktatur – Chance oder Fluch?', Leipzig, 2–4 December 1994.
3. Session entitled 'Oral History: The State of the Art', at a meeting of the *Oral History Association*, 'Memory and the Sense of Place', Philadelphia, U.S.A., 10–13 October 1995.

I. PRESS ARTICLES

Die Andere

1. 'Der Blick in die Akten: Gestohlenes Leben: Interview mit Bärbel Bohley nach zwei Tagen Lesen ihrer Stasi-Unterlagen', *Die Andere*, 9 January 1992 [n.p.].

Die Berliner Morgenpost

2. 'Gauck: Stasi-Hysterie auch Resultat geringer Vergangenheitsbewältigung', *Berliner Morgenpost*, 19 September 1991 [n.p.].
3. 'Die Angst, einen Teil der guten Erinnerung zu verlieren', *Berliner Morgenpost*, 3 January 1992 [n.p.].
4. 'Gericht gibt Bärbel Bohley in Streitsache mit Gregor Gysi recht', *Berliner Morgenpost*, 18 January 1995, p. 5.
5. 'Bärbel Bohley bittet Bundestag um Hilfe gegen Gysi: CDU ruft zur Demo auf', *Berliner Morgenpost*, 2 June 1995, p. 2.

Die Berliner Zeitung

6. 'Humanistische Union nimmt Gauck den Preis wieder weg', *Berliner Zeitung*, 14–15 December 1991 [n.p.].
7. ' "Maximillian" gab noch im Oktober '89 Spitzelbericht', *Berliner Zeitung*, 9 January 1992 [n.p.].
8. 'Willkür statt Gerechtigkeit', *Berliner Zeitung*, 21 January 1992 [n.p.].
9. ' "Stolpe-Streit beenden" ', *Berliner Zeitung*, 6 October 1992, p. 5.
10. Wolf, C., 'Eine Auskunft', *Berliner Zeitung*, 21 January 1993, p. 2.
11. 'Sollen die Archive der Stasi geschlossen werden?', *Berliner Zeitung*, 22 November 1993, p. 5.
12. 'Biermann: Die Stasi wollte mich umbringen', *Berliner Zeitung*, 1 December 1994, p. 5.

Die Frankfurter Allgemeine Zeitung

13. Schirrmacher, F., 'Hetze: Die zweite Stunde Null?', *Frankfurter Allgemeine Zeitung*, 18 June 1990, p. 31.
14. 'Warum werden wieder einmal nur die Kleinen gehängt, Professor Quaritsch?', *Frankfurter Allgemeine Zeitung – Magazin*, 18 October 1991, pp. 126–7.
15. Winters, P. J., 'Unrecht harrt des Urteils', *Frankfurter Allgemeine Zeitung*, 7 January 1992 [n.p.].
16. 'Vera Wollenberger fordert Stolpe zum Rücktritt auf', *Frankfurter Allgemeine Zeitung*, 25 August 1992, p. 1.
17. 'Vergleichsvorschlag angenommen: Sowohl Stolpe als auch Gauck fühlt sich bestätigt', *Frankfurter Allgemeine Zeitung*, 24 June 1993, p. 5.
18. Müller, C. P., 'Die Überprüfung von Lehrern in Thüringen ist schwierig, langweilig und teuer', *Frankfurter Allgemeine Zeitung*, 30 June 1993, p. 4.
19. 'Der PDS-Vorstand kritisiert Frau Kaiser', *Frankfurter Allgemeine Zeitung*, 21 September 1994, p. 6.
20. Leithäuser, J., 'Als die Bürger die Stasi-Ämter stürmten: Erinnerung zum 5. Jahrestag', *Frankfurter Allgemeine Zeitung*, 5 December 1994, p. 4.

Die Frankfurter Rundschau

21. ' "Aus heutiger Sicht war es ein Fehler, zu wenig gefragt zu haben": Eine Erklärung der Evangelischen Kirche Berlin-Brandenburg zu den Stasi-Kontakten und den Gesprächen Manfred Stolpes', *Frankfurter Rundschau*, 31 October 1992, p. 12.
22. 'Boykott des Stolpe-Ausschusses: Bürgerrechtler wollen gegen ihre späte Ladung protestieren', *Frankfurter Rundschau*, 2 March 1993, p. 1.
23. 'Neue Herren, neue Kriecher – und manchmal sind es diesselben: Stasi-Akten

vernichten oder nicht?: Ein FR-Streitgespräch zwischen Friedrich Schorlemmer und Wolfgang Templin', *Frankfurter Rundschau*, 7 December 1993, p. 20.

24. ' "Manfred Stolpe war ein Mann der Kirche, nicht des MfS" ', *Frankfurter Rundschau*, 5 April 1995, p. 20.
25. Günther, I., 'Und jetzt alle: "Gysi ist ein Stasi-Spitzel": Einstige DDR-Bürgerrechtler feiern bei Bärbel Bohley ein nostalgisches Protest-Fest', *Frankfurter Rundschau*, 9 June 1995, p. 4.
26. 'Rechtsstaatlichkeit für Gysi', *Frankfurter Rundschau*, 12 June 1995, p. 4.

Das Hallesche Tageblatt

27. Könau, S., 'Einzelfallprüfung', *Hallesches Tagesblatt*, 14 July 1994, p. 2.

Die Junge Welt

28. Ehlert, M., 'Krise auf dem Parkplatz', *Junge Welt*, 23 April 1993, p. 12.
29. 'Können wir uns einen Gauck leisten?', *Junge Welt*, 5 February 1994, p. 6.

Die Märkische Allgemeine Zeitung

30. 'Es geht ihr nicht um Schuldzuweisung', *Märkische Allgemeine Zeitung*, 26 October 1994, p. 9.

Das Neue Deutschland

31. 'Als eine "Belastete" in das Parlament?', *Neues Deutschland*, 27–8 August 1994, p. 5.
32. 'Persönliche Erklärung von Gregor Gysi zum MfS-Vorwurf', *Neues Deutschland*, 23 May 1995, p. 4.

Le Nouvel Observateur

33. 'Les mouchards de la Stasi', *le nouvel Observateur*, 15 December 1994, Dossier [n.p.].

Die Ostsee Zeitung

34. 'Gauck – Entmündigung schuf Untertanen-Mentalität', *Ostsee Zeitung*, 25 July 1994 [n.p.].

Der Spiegel

35. ' "Ehrlich, treu, zuverlässig" ', *Der Spiegel*, 10 December 1990, pp. 30–8.
36. Fuchs, J., 'Landschaften der Lüge', *Der Spiegel*, 18 November 1991, pp. 280–91.
37. ' "Ziel: Ein Intimverhältnis" ', *Der Spiegel*, 13 January 1992, p. 30.
38. ' "Sie hat nichts merken können": SPIEGEL-Reporter Jürgen Leinemann über Vera Wollenberger und ihren spitzelnden Ehemann Knud', *Der Spiegel*, 13 January 1992, pp. 34–8.
39. 'Tiefer als unter die Haut: Wolf Biermann über Schweinehunde, halbe Helden, Imitäten und andere Funde aus seinen Stasi-Akten', *Der Spiegel*, 27 January 1992, pp. 180–5.
40. Vaatz, V., ' "Die Akten lügen nicht" ', *Der Spiegel*, 27 April 1992, pp. 32–4.
41. ' "Kampf um die Seele": Wie die Stasi mit ausgefeilten Psycho-Tricks ihre Inoffiziellen Mitarbeiter anwarb und betreute', *Der Spiegel*, 27 April 1992, pp. 36–43.
42. ' "Revolutionär? Sicher nicht": Der brandenburgische Ministerpräsident Manfred Stolpe über seine Rolle im SED-Staat', *Der Spiegel*, 18 May 1992, pp. 32–6.

43. 'Putzfrau für Mielke', *Der Spiegel*, 18 May 1992, pp. 68–72.
44. Biermann, W., ' "à la lanterne! à la lanterne" ', *Der Spiegel*, 21 September 1992, pp. 81–92.
45. Weiss, K., ' "WIR MÜSSEN UNS DER WAHRHEIT STELLEN": Mythos und Stasigraphie', in 'Stasi-Akte "Verräter": Bürgerrechtler Templin: Dokumente einer Verfolgung', *Spiegel Spezial*, 1 (1993), pp. 6–9.
46. Mauz, G., 'Auf den Stufen Babylons', *Der Spiegel*, 1 November 1993, pp. 72–80.
47. ' "Des Satans Spießgesellen": Ein offener Brief des Schriftstellers Wolf Biermann an Friedrich Schorlemmer', *Der Spiegel*, 6 December 1993, pp. 42–6.
48. 'IM Rudolf grüßt IM Sekretär: SPIEGEL-Redakteur Hartmut Palmer über den Machtkampf zwischen PDS and SPD in Potsdam', *Der Spiegel*, 13 December 1993, pp. 76–7.
49. 'Politisch bedenklich', *Der Spiegel*, 7 March 1994, p. 90.
50. 'Nickis auf bloßer Haut', *Der Spiegel*, 24 October 1994, pp. 31–4.
51. ' "Ich will unser Blut zurück": Egon Bahr über den Umgang der SPD mit der PDS und die Bewältigung der DDR-Vergangenheit', *Der Spiegel*, 24 October 1994, pp. 41–7.
52. 'Gregors Berichte', *Der Spiegel*, 7 November 1994, pp. 26–30.
53. ' "Wir waren abgedriftet" ', *Der Spiegel*, 7 November 1994, pp. 40–54.
54. ' "Dann sind wir die Trottel" ', *Der Spiegel*, 21 November 1994, pp. 45–9.
55. ' "Die Täter schweigen": SPIEGEL-Streitgespräch', *Der Spiegel*, 17 April 1995, pp. 92–4.
56. 'Deckname "Leitz" ', *Der Spiegel*, 22 May 1995, pp. 87–8.
57. Schmitz, M., 'Zum zweitenmal betrogen', *Der Spiegel*, 30 October 1995, pp. 40–2.
58. Walther, J., ' "Im stinkenden Untergrund" ', *Der Spiegel*, 23 September 1996, pp. 224–33.

Die Süddeutsche Zeitung

59. 'Stolpe räumt Fehler bei Stasi-Aufarbeitung ein', *Süddeutsche Zeitung*, 5 April 1994, p. 5.
60. 'Stasi-Überprüfung begrenzt', *Süddeutsche Zeitung*, 9–10 November 1996, p. 2.

Der Tagesspiegel

61. Schorlemmer, F., 'Gerichte reichen nicht: Ein Tribunal ist vonnöten', *Der Tagesspiegel*, 13 September 1991 [n.p.].
62. 'Ein kleiner aber heftiger Streit: Diskussionsabend in der Gauck-Behörde über "das schwierige Erbe" ', *Der Tagesspiegel*, 25 September 1993, p. 4.
63. 'Kontroverse über Äußerungen Kohls zu den Stasi-Akten', *Der Tagesspiegel*, 5 November 1993, p. 1.
64. Maroldt, L., 'Vergeblicher Wunsch nach inhaltlicher Tiefe', *Der Tagesspiegel*, 22 September 1994, p. 3.

Die Tageszeitung

65. 'Die Stasi war gefährlich, dilettantisch und prüde', *die tageszeitung*, 4 January 1992 [n.p.].

66. Giordano, R., 'Wider falsche Barmherzigkeit im Fall Erich Honecker', *die tageszeitung*, 23 November 1992, p. 10.
67. Thierse, W., ' "Ich habe nicht so viele Gewißheiten" ', *die tageszeitung*, 5 May 1994, p. 12.
68. Fuchs, J., ' "Wo angekommen?" ', *die tageszeitung*, 5 May 1994, p. 12.
69. 'Juristischer Erfolg für Gregor Gysi', *die tageszeitung*, 20–21 May 1995, p. 2.
70. Gast, W., ' "Spezialvariante für Gysi": Joachim Gauck, Bundesbeauftragter für die Stasi-Unterlagen, zum Gutachten über Gregor Gysi', *die tageszeitung*, 12 June 1995, p. 10.

Die Welt

71. 'Schmerzensgeld für den Mann, den sein Neffe verriet', *Die Welt*, 21 April 1995, p. B1.

Die Wochenpost

72. Mehr, M. T., 'Abschied von der Diktatur: Ein Gespräch mit Jürgen Fuchs über Täter, Opfer und Stasi-Akten', *Die Wochenpost*, 12 March 1992 [n.p.].
73. ' ". . . dann schlägt die Vergangenheit zurück": Joachim Gauck über Verdrängung, falsche Solidarität mit den Tätern und das Leben in der DDR', *Die Wochenpost*, 25 February 1993, pp. 30–1.
74. Reich, J., 'Spätsommer '93 – Deutschland', *Die Wochenpost*, 30 September 1993, pp. 50–1.
75. Engler, W., 'Die kleine Freiheit', *Die Wochenpost*, 10 March 1994, pp. 30–3.
76. Gauck, J., 'Über Zivilcourage: Die beschwerliche Freiheit und das süße Gift der Abhängigkeit', *Die Wochenpost*, 3 November 1994, p. 11.

Die Zeit

77. Honecker, E., 'Worte der Woche', *Die Zeit*, 23 February 1990, p. 2.
78. Biermann, W., 'Auch ich war bei der Stasi', *Die Zeit*, 4 May 1990, pp. 73–5.
79. Radisch, I., 'Das ist nicht so einfach: Ein ZEIT-Gespräch mit Sascha Anderson', *Die Zeit*, 1 November 1991, pp. 65–6.
80. Habermas, J., 'Bemerkungen zu einer verworrenen Diskussion: Was bedeutet "Aufarbeitung der Vergangenheit heute?" ', *Die Zeit*, 3 April 1992, pp. 82–4.
81. Sommer, T., ' "Der lange Atem der Wahrheit": Brandenburgs Ministerpräsident im ZEIT-Gespräch: Ist das Verfahren der Gauck-Behörde rechtsstaatlich zu verkraften?', *Die Zeit*, 17 April 1992, p. 3.
82. Reich, J., 'Am DDRreizehnten Grad östlicher Länge', *Die Zeit*, 12 November 1993, p. 60.
83. Müller, H., 'Das Ticken der Norm', *Die Zeit*, 14 January 1994, pp. 49–50.
84. Frenkl, R., 'Die DDR vor Gericht', *Die Zeit*, 21 January 1994, p. 40.
85. Heym, S., 'Worte der Woche', *Die Zeit*, 25 February 1994, p. 2.
86. Nawrocki, J., 'Streit ums Ungewisse', *Die Zeit*, 18 March 1994, p. 8.
87. Leicht, R., 'Moral gegen Macht: Doppelte Bilanz: Der Fall Stolpe und die SED-Diktatur', *Die Zeit*, 24 June 1994, p. 1.
88. Leicht, R., 'Zur Person', *Die Zeit*, 9 September 1994, p. 1.
89. ' "Gregor Gysi hat durch seine Tätigkeit als Anwalt eine der größten Karrieren im Lügen- Bespitzelungs- und Unrechtssystem der DDR gemacht" ', *Die Zeit*, 27 October 1994, p. 2.
90. Reich, J., 'Weich abgewickelt', *Die Zeit*, 9 December 1994, p. 7.

91. Wesel, U., 'Plädoyer für ein Schlußgesetz', *Die Zeit*, 6 January 1995, p. 3.
92. Dönhoff, M. G., 'Gerechtigkeit ist nicht Vergeltung', *Die Zeit*, 12 January 1995, p. 1.
93. Eörsi, I., 'Mit der Lüge leben', *Die Zeit*, 3 March 1995, p. 10.
94. Dinescu, M., 'Die Akten bleiben im Schrank', *Die Zeit*, 24 March 1995, p. 16.
95. Harting, K., 'Wenn die alte Heimat verlorengeht', *Die Zeit*, 27 December 1996, p. 2.

J. SECONDARY LITERATURE

1. 'Entscheidungen: Öffentliche Äußerungen des Bundesbeauftragten für die Stasi-Unterlagen', *Neue Juristische Woche*, 39 (1993), 2548–52.
2. 'Quelle: IM »Gerhard«', in J-14, pp. 242–9.
3. 'Rechtssprechung: Publikation von Stasi-Akten im öffentlichen Interesse ("Kant/Kunze")', *Deutsch-Deutsche Rechtszeitschrift*, 11 (1993), 349–51.
4. Anz, T., ed., *'Es geht nicht um Christa Wolf': Der Literaturstreit im vereinten Deutschland*. Munich: edition spangenberg, 1991.
5. Behnke, K. and Fuchs, J., eds., *Zersetzung der Seele: Psychologie und Psychiatrie im Dienste der Stasi*. Hamburg: Rotbuch, 1995.
6. Beleites, M., *Untergrund: Ein Konflikt mit der Stasi in der Uran-Provinz*. Berlin: BasisDruck, 1992.
7. Bertaux, D., 'From the Life History Approach to the Transformation of Sociological Practice', in J-9, pp. 29–45.
8. Bertaux, D., and Bertaux-Wiame, I., 'Life Stories in the Baker's Trade', in J-9, pp. 169–89.
9. Bertaux, D., ed., *Biography and Society: The Life History Approach in the Social Sciences*. Beverly Hills: SAGE, 1981.
10. Biermann, W., 'Der Lichtblick im gräßlichen Fatalismus der Geschichte: Rede zur Verleihung des Georg-Büchner-Preises', in J-14, pp. 298–304.
11. Biermann, W., 'Nur wer sich ändert, bleibt sich treu', in J-4, pp. 139–56.
12. Bodi, L., 'Intellectuals, Writers and the Stasi Files', *MEANJIN*, 52 (1993), 7–22.
13. Bohley, B., 'Die Macht wird entzaubert', in J-76, pp. 38–46.
14. Böthig, P. and Michael, K., eds., *Machtspiele: Literatur und Staatssicherheit*. Leipzig: Reclam, 1993.
15. Bourdieu, P., *Sociology in Question*. London: SAGE, 1993.
16. Broder, H. M., *Erbarmen mit den Deutschen*. Hamburg: Hoffmann und Campe, 1994.
17. Broderson, I., ed., *Joachim Gauck: Die Stasi-Akten, Das unheimliche Erbe der DDR*. Reinbek: Rowohlt, 1991.
18. Browning, C., *Ordinary Men: Reserve Police Battalion 101 and the Final Solution in Poland*. New York: HarperCollins, 1992.
19. Derrida, J., *Gesetzeskraft: Der mythische 'Grund der Autorität'*. Frankfurt/Main: Suhrkamp, 1991.
20. Dönhoff, M. G., Introduction to J-21, pp. 7–14.
21. Dönhoff, M., et al., *Weil das Land Versöhnung braucht: Ein Manifest II*. Reinbek: Rowohlt, 1993.

22. Engelmann, R., 'Zum Quellenwert der Unterlagen des Ministeriums für Staatssicherheit', in J-34, pp. 23–39.
23. Eppelmann, R., *Fremd im eigenen Haus: Mein Leben im anderen Deutschland*. Cologne: Kiepenheuer und Witsch, 1993.
24. Fricke, K. W., Lechner, H., and Thysen, U., *Errungenschaften und Legenden: Runder Tisch, Willkürherrschaft und Kommandowirtschaft im DDR-Sozialismus*. Melle: Knoth, 1990.
25. Fricke, K. W., *MfS intern: Macht, Strukturen, Auflösung der DDR-Staatssicherheit*. Cologne: Wissenschaft und Politik, 1991.
26. Fuchs, J., *. . . und wann kommt der Hammer?: Psychologie, Opposition und Staatssicherheit*. Berlin: BasisDruck, 1990.
27. Fuchs, J., 'Bearbeiten, dirigieren, zuspitzen: Die "leisen" Methoden des MfS', in J-5, pp. 44–83.
28. Fuchs, J., *Gedächtnisprotokolle, Vernehmuhngsprotokolle: November '76 bis September '77*. Reinbek: Rowohlt, 1990.
29. Gill, D. and Schröter, U., *Das Ministerium für Staatssicherheit: Anatomie des Mielke-Imperiums*. Berlin: Rowohlt, 1991.
30. Goldhagen, D. J., *Hitler's Willing Executioners: Ordinary Germans and the Holocaust*. London: Little, Brown and Company, 1996.
31. Grass, G., *Ein Schnäppchen namens DDR: Letzte Reden vorm Glockengeläut*. Frankfurt/Main: Luchterhand, 1990.
32. Grele, R. J., *Envelopes of Sound: The Art of Oral History*, 2nd edn. New York: Praeger, 1991.
33. Heidelberger-Leonard, I., ed., *Jurek Becker*. Frankfurt/Main: Suhrkamp, 1992.
34. Henke, K.-D. and Engelmann, R., eds., *Aktenlage: Die Bedeutung der Unterlagen des Staatssicherheitsdienstes für die Zeitgeschichtsforschung*. Berlin: Ch. Links, 1995.
35. Henke, K.-D., ed., *Wann bricht schon mal ein Staat zusammen!: Die Debatte über die Stasi-Akten auf dem 39. Historikertag 1992*. Munich: dtv, 1993.
36. Heym, S., *Filz: Gedanken über das neuste Deutschland*. Frankfurt/Main: Fischer, 1994.
37. Hugler, K., *Missbrauchtes Vertrauen: Christliche Jugendarbeit unter den Augen der Stasi*. Neukirchen-Vluyn: Aussat, 1994.
38. Jackson, P., ed., *DDR – Das Ende eines Staates*. Manchester: Manchester University Press, 1994.
39. Karau, G., *Stasiprotokolle: Gespräche mit ehemaligen Mitarbeitern des 'Ministeriums für Staatssicherheit' der DDR*. Frankfurt/Main: dipa, 1992.
40. Kinkel, K., from a speech given on 9 July 1991, in '40 Jahre SED–Unrecht – eine Herausforderung für den Rechtsstaat, insbesondere das Strafrecht: Erstes Forum des Bundesministers der Justiz am 9. Juli 1991 in Bonn', *Zeitschrift für Gesetzgebung*, Special Edition 2. Munich: C. H. Beck, 1991, 4–8.
41. Kleinschmid, H., 'Der Mut zum Nein: Ein Bericht über Menschen, die sich der Stasi verweigerten', *Deutschland Archiv*, 4 (1995), 348–59.
42. Klüger, R., *Weiter leben: Eine Jugend*, 3rd edn. Munich: dtv, 1995.
43. Kohli, M., 'Biography: Account, Text, Method', in J-9, pp. 61–75.
44. Körzendörfer, M., 'Mehr Schein als Sein', *Weibblick*, 16 (1994), 26–8.

45. Kukutz, I. and Havemann, K., *Geschützte Quelle: Gespräche mit Monika H. alias Karin Lenz*. Berlin: BasisDruck, 1990.
46. Kunert, G., 'Meine Nachbarn', in J-76, pp. 47–50.
47. Kunert, G., 'Selbstflüchtigkeit', in J-72, pp. 16–24.
48. Kunze, R., *Deckname 'Lyrik'*. Frankfurt/Main: Fischer, 1990.
49. Lahann, B., *Genosse Judas: Die zwei Leben des Ibrahim Böhme*. Reinbek: Rowohlt, 1992.
50. Lansnicker, F. and Schwirtzek, T., 'Staatssicherheit und öffentlicher Dienst', *Neue Jurisitische Woche*, 4 (1993), 106–10.
51. Lepenies, W., *Folgen einer unerhörten Begebenheit: Die Deutschen nach der Vereinigung*. Berlin: Siedler, 1992.
52. Loest, E., *Die Stasi war mein Eckermann; oder, Mein leben mit der Wanze*. Leipzig: Linden, 1991.
53. Maaz, H.-J., *Das gestürzte Volk: Die unglückliche Einheit*. Berlin: Argon, 1991.
54. Maaz, H.-J., *Der Gefühlsstau: Ein Psychogramm der DDR*. Munich: Knaur, 1992.
55. Maaz, H.-J., *Die Entrüstung: Deutschland, Deutschland, Stasi, Schuld und Sündenbock*. Berlin: Argon, 1992.
56. Melle, F. H., 'I.M.', in J-14, pp. 144–62.
57. Mitscherlich, A. and Mitscherlich, M., *Die Unfähigkeit zu trauern: Grundlage kollektiven Verhaltens*. Munich: Piper, 1967.
58. Mitscherlich-Nielson, M., 'Die (Un)Fähigkeit zu trauern in Ost- und Westdeutschland: Was Trauerarbeit heißen könnte', *Psyche*, 46 (1992), 406–18.
59. Mitter, A. and Wolle, S., *Untergang auf Raten: Unbekannte Kapitel der DDR-Geschichte*. Munich: C. Bertelsmann, 1993.
60. Morris, H., *On Guilt and Innocence: Essays in Legal Philosophy and Moral Psychology*. Berkeley: University of California Press, 1976.
61. Morris, P. and Gruneberg, M., eds., *Theoretical Aspects of Memory*, 2nd edn. London: Routledge, 1994.
62. Müller-Enbergs, H., *Inoffizielle Mitarbeiter des Ministeriums für Staatssicherheit: Richtlinien und Durchführungsbestimmungen*. Berlin: Ch. Links, 1996.
63. Müller-Enbergs, H., 'Warum wird einer IM?: Zur Motivation bei der inoffiziellen Zusammenarbeit mit dem Staatssicherheitsdienst', in J-5, pp. 102–29.
64. Müller-Enbergs, H., 'Zum Verhältnis von Norm und Praxis in der Arbeit mit Inoffiziellen Mitarbeitern des Ministeriums für Staatssicherheit', in J-34, pp. 56–76.
65. Noll, C., *Nachtgedanken über Deutschland*. Reinbek: Rowohlt, 1992.
66. Perks, R., *Oral History: Talking about the Past*. London: The Historical Association, 1992.
67. Portelli, A., 'The Peculiarities of Oral History', *History Workshop*, 12 (1981), 96–107.
68. Rathenow, L., 'Die Zeit heilt gar nichts: Vom Umgang mit den Stasi-Akten', *Blätter für deutsche und internationale Politik*, 12 (1990), 1461–68.
69. Rathenow, L., 'Teile zu keinem Bild; oder, Das Puzzle von der geheimen Macht', in J-76, pp. 62–90.
70. Reuth, R. G., IM *Sekretär: Die 'Gauck-Recherche' und die Dokumente zum 'Fall Stolpe'*. Berlin: Ullstein, 1992.

71. Riecker, A., Schwarz, A. and Schneider, D., eds., *Stasi intim: Gespräche mit ehemaligen MfS-Mitarbeitern*. Leipzig: Forum, 1990.
72. Rietzchel, T., ed., *Über Deutschland: Schriftsteller geben Auskunft*. Leipzig: Reclam, 1993.
73. Rosenberg, T., *The Haunted Land: Facing Europe's Ghosts after Communism*. New York: Random House, 1995.
74. Ross, M., 'Relation of Implicit Theories to the Construction of Personal Histories', *Psychological Review*, 96 (1989), 341–57.
75. Ross, M. and Conway, M., 'Remembering One's Own Past: The Construction of Personal Histories', in J-89, pp. 122–44.
76. Schädlich, H. J., ed., *Aktenkundig*. Berlin: Rowohlt, 1992.
77. Schedlinski, R., 'Die Unzuständigkeit der Macht', *Neue Deutsche Literatur*, 474 (1992), 75–105.
78. Schirrmacher, F., 'Verdacht und Verrat: Die Stasi-Vergangenheit verändert die literarische Szene', in J-14, pp. 304–8.
79. Schlesinger, K., 'Macht, Literatur, Staatssicherheit', *Text und Kritik*, 120 (1993), 29–35.
80. Schmidt, A., 'Gegenstrategien: Über die Möglichkeiten, sich zu verweigern', in J-5, pp. 158–77.
81. Schorlemmer, F., *Bis alle Mauern fallen: Texte aus einem verschwundenen Land*. Munich: Knaur, 1993.
82. Schorlemmer, F., *Versöhnung mit der Wahrheit: Nachschläge und Vorschläge eines Ostdeutschen*. Munich: Knaur, 1992.
83. Schröder, H., 'Identität, Individualität und psychische Befindlichkeit des DDR-Bürgers im Umbruch', *Zeitschrift für Sozialisationsforschung und Erziehungssoziologie*, Special Edition 1 (1990), 163–76.
84. Schröder, H., 'Staatliche Repression und psychische Folgen', *Gruppendynamik*, 4 (1990), 341–56.
85. Schröder, H., 'Zur psychologischen Vergangenheitsbewältigung der DDR-Bürger nach der Wende', *Psychosozial*, 45 (1991), 23–9.
86. Schröder, R., '. . . und wie soll es weitergehen?', in J-21, pp. 121–5.
87. Schröter, U., 'Die Spannbreite der IM-Tätigkeit', *Zwie Gespräch*, 23 (1994), 1–13.
88. Sinakowski, A., *Das Verhör*. Berlin: BasisDruck, 1991.
89. Sorrentino, R. M. and Higgins, E. T., eds., *Handbook of Motivation and Cognition: Foundations of Social Behaviour*. Chichester: Wiley, 1986.
90. Smith, S. M., 'Theoretical Principles of Context-Dependent Memory', in J-61, pp. 168–95.
91. Stolpe, M., *Schwieriger Aufbruch*. Berlin: Siedler, 1992.
92. Sühl, K., ed., *Vergangenheitsbewältigung 1945 und 1989: Ein unmöglicher Vergleich?, Eine Diskussion*. Berlin: Volk und Welt, 1994.
93. Süß, W., ' "Schild und Schwert": Das Ministerium für Staatssicherheit und die SED', in J-34, pp. 83–97.
94. Szczypiorski, A., 'Die Deutschen quälen sich mit der Vergangenheit: Gespräch über die Stasi und die Pflichten der geistigen Elite', in J-14, pp. 367–72.
95. Thierse, W., 'Mut zur eigenen Geschichte: Lehren aus der Vergangenheit', in J-92, pp. 19–36.

96. Thomas, W. I. and Znaniecki, F., *The Polish Peasant in Europe and America*, 2 vols. New York: Dover, 1958 [first published 1918–20].
97. Thompson, P., 'Life Histories and the Analysis of Social Change', in J-9, pp. 289–306.
98. Thompson, P., *The Voice of the Past: Oral History*, 2nd edn. Oxford: Oxford University Press, 1988.
99. Vinke, H., ed., *Akteneinsicht Christa Wolf: Zerrspiegel und Dialog, Eine Dokumentation*. Hamburg: Luchterhand, 1993.
100. Walther, J., *Sicherungsbereich Literatur: Schriftsteller und Staatssicherheit in der Deutschen Demokratischen Republik*. Berlin: Ch. Links, 1996.
101. Wawrzyn, L., *Der Blaue: Das Spitzelsystem der DDR*. Berlin: Wagenbach, 1990.
102. Wedel, M., *Einheitsfrust*. Berlin: Rowohlt, 1994.
103. Winograd, E., 'Naturalistic Approaches to Memory Study', in J-61, pp. 273–95.
104. Wolf, C., *Was bleibt: Erzählung*. Frankfurt/Main: Luchterhand, 1990.
105. Wolle, S., 'In the Labyrinth of the Documents: The Archival Legacy of the SED-State', *German History*, 10 (1992), 352–65.
106. Wolle, S., 'The poisoned society: The Stasi file syndrome in the former GDR', *History Workshop*, 33 (1992), 138–44.
107. Wollenberger, V., 'Eine zweite Vergewaltigung', in J-76, pp. 154–65.
108. Wollenberger, V., *Virus der Heuchler: Innenansicht aus Stasi-Akten*. Berlin: Elefantenpress, 1992.
109. Worst, A., *Das Ende eines Geheimdienstes; oder, Wie lebendig ist die Stasi?* Berlin: LinksDruck, 1991.
110. Zulind, B., *Deckname 'Sonnenblume': Das unverwechselbare Leben einer Rollstuhlfahrerin in der DDR*. Berlin: Frieling, 1993.

INDEX